GOD CALLS YOU WORTHY, Girl

Janice Thompson

GOD CALLS YOU WORTHY, Girl

180 DEVOTIONS & PRAYERS for Teens

BARBOUR
PUBLISHING

Scripture quotations marked NCV are taken from the New Century Version®. Copyright © 2005 by Thomas Nelson. Used by permission. All rights reserved.

Scripture quotations marked NLV are taken from the New Life Version copyright © 1969 and 2003. Used by Barbour Publishing, Inc., Uhrichsville, Ohio, 44683. All rights reserved.

Scripture quotations marked NIV are taken from the HOLY BIBLE, NEW INTERNATIONAL VERSION®, NIV®. Copyright © 1973, 1978, 1984, 2011 by Biblica, Inc.® Used by permission of Zondervan. All rights reserved worldwide. www.zondervan.com. The "NIV" and "New International Version" are trademarks registered in the United States Patent and Trademark Office by Biblica, Inc.®

Scripture quotations marked TLB are taken from The Living Bible copyright © 1971 by Tyndale House Foundation. Used by permission of Tyndale House Publishers, Carol Stream, Illinois 60188. All rights reserved.

Scripture quotations marked CEV are taken from the Contemporary English Version, Copyright © 1995 by American Bible Society. All rights reserved.

Scripture quotations marked GW are taken from GOD'S WORD®. Copyright © 1995, 2003, 2013, 2014, 2019, 2020 by God's Word to the Nations Mission Society. All rights reserved.

Scripture quotations marked ESV are taken from The Holy Bible, English Standard Version® (ESV®). Copyright © 2001 by Crossway, a publishing ministry of Good News Publishers. All rights reserved.

Scripture quotations marked NLT are taken from the *Holy Bible*, New Living Translation, copyright © 1996, 2004, 2015 by Tyndale House Foundation. Used by permission of Tyndale House Publishers, Carol Stream, Illinois 60188. All rights reserved.

Scripture quotations marked MSG are taken from THE MESSAGE, copyright © 1993, 2002, 2018 by Eugene H. Peterson. Used by permission of NavPress, represented by Tyndale House Publishers. All rights reserved.

Scripture quotations marked KJV are taken from the King James Version of the Bible.

Published by Barbour Publishing, Inc., 1810 Barbour Drive, Uhrichsville, Ohio 44683, www.barbourbooks.com

Our mission is to inspire the world with the life-changing message of the Bible.

Member of the
Evangelical Christian
Publishers Association

Printed in China.

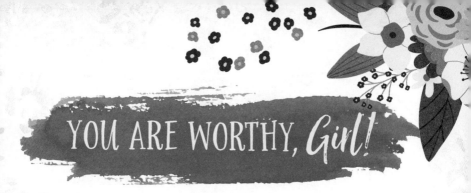

YOU ARE WORTHY, *Girl!*

Have you ever reached the end of a challenge and had someone ask you, "Well? Was it worth it? Was it worth all the pain, the agony, the work, to reach the finish line?" No doubt you responded with a hearty *yes!* When something is "worth" it, the investment pays off.

Girl, God wants you to know that you are worth it. You're worth the trip to the cross that Jesus made. You're worth the time and effort He puts into shaping you into a godly young woman. You're worth it—not because of anything you've done but simply because you're His child.

Does it bring a sense of relief to know you don't have to work overtime to earn the favor of your heavenly Father? Nothing you do—or don't do—will change your worth. Before you ever came into this world, He saw you as worthy of being created in His image.

You're worth it. And He wants you to know that right from the start! So allow these devotions to convince you, one day at a time, that you have great value to God and to His people.

"Indeed, the very hairs of your head are all numbered. Don't be afraid; you are worth more than many sparrows."
LUKE 12:7 NIV

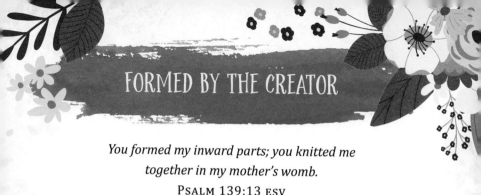

FORMED BY THE CREATOR

You formed my inward parts; you knitted me
together in my mother's womb.
PSALM 139:13 ESV

Have you ever stopped to think about what your life was like before you were born? When you were tucked away in your mother's womb, you had value. Even then, you were precious to God.

Your awesome heavenly Father took the time to craft every part of you, long before you made your entrance into this world. Your skin, personality, and even your fingernails were all taking shape as He spun you into existence. Even then, God knew whether your hair would be curly or straight, whether you'd be short or tall, and what quirks you would have. (After all, He designed you to be unique!)

You had value then, and you have value now. Your worth isn't determined by anything you might do, though it's great to act right. You're great because the Greatest Single Force in the universe took the time to make you! (Think about a master craftsman carving a delicate piece of furniture. It's worth a lot more because it's handmade.)

You're handmade, girl. You were crafted on purpose, *for* a purpose. And God adored you even before your mama knew she was expecting you.

Thank You for loving me from the
very beginning, Jesus! Amen.

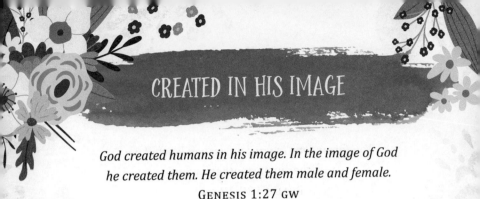

CREATED IN HIS IMAGE

God created humans in his image. In the image of God
he created them. He created them male and female.
GENESIS 1:27 GW

Have you ever taken a photo of a friend and tried to turn it into a sketch? Making a replica isn't easy! Rarely does the copy end up looking like the original.

Girl, you look like the original. You were created in the image of God, and you look like Him. You've got His DNA. Your personality, your quirkiness, the way you talk, these are all things you got from Him.

You have a "true likeness" to the original. And because you were created in His image (an amazing replica), you're part of Him. He's your Father. And your heavenly Father thinks you're all that and a bag of chips! You're His kid, after all.

Parents love their kids, and this is especially true with God. He stays up nights trying to think of ways to bless you. And nothing you do—not even the worst thing—will change His opinion of you, though He is especially proud when you set a great example.

You're worthy, girl. Your Daddy says so.

Thank You for creating me in Your image, Lord! Amen.

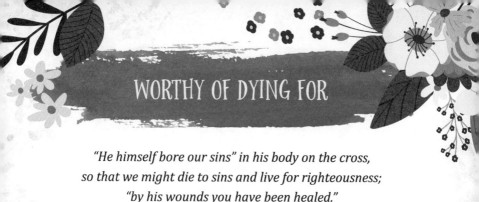

WORTHY OF DYING FOR

*"He himself bore our sins" in his body on the cross,
so that we might die to sins and live for righteousness;
"by his wounds you have been healed."*
1 PETER 2:24 NIV

If someone came to you and said, "Hey, I've got an idea. This really bad man in prison—the one who murdered someone—is scheduled for execution. Here's my idea: I think you should die in his place so that he can live."

Would you agree? Um, probably not! It's one thing to lay down your life for someone you know and love; it's another thing altogether to offer your life for someone wicked.

And yet, that's just what the Master Artist did for mankind. He died for everyone: the good, the bad, and the horrible. His sacrifice on the cross covered every sin that could ever be committed. And when evil people turn to Him and accept His sacrifice, they are wiped clean. Forgiven. No, *really.*

It's impossible to fathom the kind of love that sent Jesus to the cross, but here's the long and short of it: He thought you were worth it. He thought we were all worth it. And though it took every bit of strength in Him, He never regretted that decision.

I can't even imagine what You went through, Jesus. Thank You for dying for me. Amen.

MORE VALUABLE THAN SPARROWS

As you come to him, a living stone rejected by men
but in the sight of God chosen and precious. . .
1 Peter 2:4 esv

Do you ever wonder how store owners decide how much to charge for their merchandise? Who decided that a cell phone would cost hundreds of dollars? And who came up with the idea of selling things like pet rocks? (Really? Paying money for a rock?)

Back in the day, people drank water from their kitchen faucets. They didn't pay for it in bottles. It didn't come pouring out the front of their fridge. But someone decided bottled water was a high-dollar item and put it up for sale!

When it comes to assigning value, no one does a better job than God. He looked at mankind—starting with Adam and Eve—and decided they had more value than anything else He had created. More than the zebras. More than the twinkling stars. More than the ocean waves. Even more than puppies and kittens.

You, girl, are His most valuable creation. When He looks at you, He says, "This one is a top-dollar item!"

Lord, thank You for finding value in me.
That makes my heart so happy! Amen.

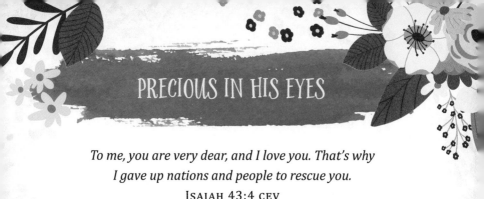

PRECIOUS IN HIS EYES

To me, you are very dear, and I love you. That's why
I gave up nations and people to rescue you.
ISAIAH 43:4 CEV

Who's your favorite person—right now, at this very moment? Of all the people on the planet, who came to mind right away as you read those words? Your BFF? Your mom? A kid sister? That guy you have a crush on?

The love that you have for that person doesn't even come close to the intense feelings your heavenly Father has for you. He's nuts about you. He believes you're far more valuable than gold or silver and even more precious than rubies or diamonds. If you lined up all of the jewelry in the world, it wouldn't come close to your value. Wow!

God would split heaven and earth wide open to care for you, girl. His love for you is that deep. He sacrificed everything, even His Son, so He could prove that love. Rest easy in knowing your heavenly Father is flipping out over you, His child.

I have to admit, I don't always feel very "precious," Jesus. Some days I'm just not feeling worthy at all. I don't know why You love me like You do, but I'm so grateful. Amen.

HE PLANS TO STICK AROUND

"Have I not commanded you? Be strong and courageous.
Do not be frightened, and do not be dismayed, for the
LORD your God is with you wherever you go."
JOSHUA 1:9 ESV

God isn't going anywhere. He won't ever abandon you. Oh sure, people take off. That guy who broke your heart? *Sayonara.* That friend who betrayed you? She didn't stick around long, did she? But God? Girl, He's not leaving you. Even on your worst day, when you're totally not feeling it, He won't abandon you. He won't leave you hanging.

Wherever you go, He's going too. Whatever job you have in front of you, He'll be right there to help you through it.

Why does your heavenly Father stick around? Why doesn't He get frustrated when you mess up? Because you're His kid. You're His own flesh and blood. And He's not going to give up on you, even on the days when you're ready to give up on yourself.

God is like superglue. You can't shake Him, so don't even try. Just rest easy, knowing He actually wants to be with you, no matter what.

Thanks for sticking with me, Jesus!
You must really love me a lot. Amen.

HE'S LOOKING AT YOUR HEART

The Lord said to Samuel, "Don't judge by a man's face or height, for this is not the one. I don't make decisions the way you do! Men judge by outward appearance, but I look at a man's thoughts and intentions."

1 SAMUEL 16:7 TLB

Today's Bible story is about King David. Well, let's back up. He wasn't a king yet. He was just a boy. The prophet Samuel was instructed by God to choose the future king for the nation of Israel. He took a close look at David's older brothers, who were bigger and better suited for the job. But, in the end, Samuel chose the little shepherd boy. (No doubt David's father was confused! "Hello? What about my older boys?")

Let's face it: the world judges by appearance. The pretty girls? Yeah, they get the attention. The handsome boys? They're the ones all the girls drool over. But the "average" ones? Many times, they get overlooked. It stinks, especially because you've already discovered that looks aren't the important thing.

But back to David. He was just a kid. But Samuel, led by the Spirit of God, saw extraordinary potential in him. And he chose David for the highest office in the land!

God sees potential in you too! He sees your value, even when others do not. (He's pretty cool like that!)

Thanks for seeing more than just the physical, Lord! Amen.

YOU'RE WONDERFULLY MADE

Thank you for making me so wonderfully complex!
It is amazing to think about. Your workmanship
is marvelous—and how well I know it.
PSALM 139:14 TLB

If you've ever been to an art museum, you know that there are some skilled artists out there. Some have a real gift for painting and sketching.

God is the best artist of all. He's ten thousand light-years better than Monet, Rembrandt, Michelangelo, or even Leonardo da Vinci. And, girl, you are His work of art! No, you're not hanging on a wall in a museum (thank goodness, right?), but you're on full display for all to see. You're fearfully and wonderfully made. The Master Artist didn't just slap you together with cheap paint. No, He used top-notch materials and took His time crafting every little thing about you.

Before you beat yourself up over how you look, before you grumble and complain about your body parts, remember that the Artist of all artists worked a *l-o-n-g* time on you, and He's pretty proud of His work!

I get it, Lord! I need to stop cutting myself down. You are an amazing Artist. I'll stop knocking Your work! Amen.

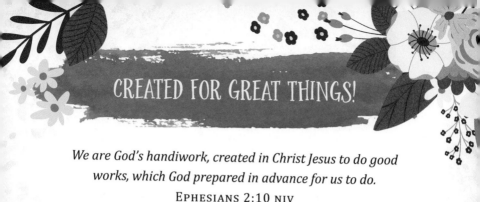

CREATED FOR GREAT THINGS!

We are God's handiwork, created in Christ Jesus to do good works, which God prepared in advance for us to do.
EPHESIANS 2:10 NIV

Girl, you were created *for* a purpose and *with* a purpose. Stop to think about those words for a minute. God didn't just plunk you down on earth for no reason. (What would be the point of that?) He specifically designed you, put you here at exactly this time frame, so that you could make a difference.

He could've chosen to make you male instead of female. He might've opted to drop you into the eighteenth century. He could've made you thinner or chubbier or given you a completely different skin tone. But He didn't. He worked His magic and came up with you—just as you are—and said, "This one needs to go in the twenty-first century. She'll accomplish great things!"

What handiwork He displays through you! (Did it ever occur to you that God might be showing off a little by putting you on display to the world?) He chose you. And you, girl, are going to do great things for Him!

Lord, I was created for a purpose and with a purpose!
I love those words. Thanks for working so hard on me.
(And thanks for choosing the twenty-first century!) Amen.

GOD ONLY SPEAKS THE TRUTH

This is he who came by water and blood—Jesus Christ; not by the water only but by the water and the blood. And the Spirit is the one who testifies, because the Spirit is the truth.

1 JOHN 5:6 ESV

You look in the mirror and groan. You hate the pimples. You can't stand your eyebrows. You wish your lips were fuller. And that hair! You'd change *everything* about it. Why can't you have great hair like the other girls?

When you stare at your reflection, you may not feel beautiful. In fact, you may not feel remotely pretty. But God's Word says you are! Consider these words from Song of Solomon 4:7: "You are altogether beautiful, my love; there is no flaw in you" (ESV). When God looks at you, He sees His beautiful daughter, cleansed and set free, thanks to the work that Jesus did on the cross.

You're beautiful. Even on the days when you're not feeling it. You're beautiful because He says so, and your amazing heavenly Father doesn't lie. In fact, He only *ever* speaks the truth. So, if He said it, it is 100 percent true.

You find me beautiful, Lord? Wow! I don't understand how, especially on the days when I'm looking rough. But Your Word says that You only tell the truth, so I'll have to believe You on this one, even when I'm not feeling it. Amen.

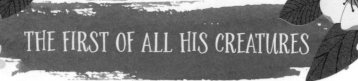

THE FIRST OF ALL HIS CREATURES

He gave us our new lives through the truth of His Word only because He wanted to. We are the first children in His family.
JAMES 1:18 NLV

If God lined up all of His creation in order of importance, guess who would be at the front of the line? You, girl! Well, you and all of the other human beings. People get the first spot in the line because God created them in His image.

He didn't create frogs in His image. Or sharks. Trees, bushes, clouds . . .they do not reflect the image of a holy God. Neither do the fish in the sea or the birds flying overhead. And none of those things have souls either. But you? You're His masterpiece, made to look and act like Him. And you've got a soul inside of you. It's the perfect dwelling place for God's Spirit, which sets you apart from the rest of creation.

So don't start cutting yourself down! Whenever you feel like you're less than, remember that you're really more than ten billion other amazing things God made.

Thanks for putting me at the front of the line, Jesus! I don't always feel like I deserve the top spot, but You do! I'm grateful for Your love. Amen.

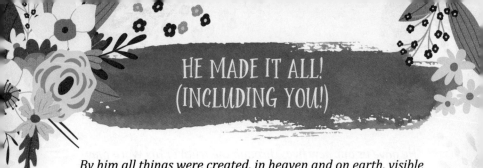

HE MADE IT ALL! (INCLUDING YOU!)

By him all things were created, in heaven and on earth, visible and invisible, whether thrones or dominions or rulers or authorities—all things were created through him and for him.

COLOSSIANS 1:16 ESV

Imagine you walk into a house. You see all of the furniture, the rugs, the paintings on the walls. You see the people, the pets, the food on the table. You see the clocks, the microwave, and the refrigerator. And, in most cases, every single one of those "things" is made by a different manufacturer. How weird would it be to walk into a house and find out that (literally) every single thing was made by one company?

Now, think about God. He created everything that would ever be necessary to make that rug. And that clock. And those paintings. He created the humans and the pets, but He also created foods and trees and all of the things that would one day become meals. And tables. And chairs. And refrigerators.

He made it all. No other "manufacturer" can boast that. But everything that is—it all exists because of God. And to think, He thought the world needed one of you too!

You're amazing, God! By You all things were created— the things we see and the things we can't. Wow! Amen.

HE KNOWS YOU, INSIDE AND OUT

O Lord, You have looked through me and have known me. You know when I sit down and when I get up. You understand my thoughts from far away. You look over my path and my lying down. You know all my ways very well. Even before I speak a word, O Lord, You know it all.
PSALM 139:1–4 NLV

God knows you. He knows every little quirky thing about you. He knows when you're mad. He knows when you're sad. He's completely clued in when you're having a bad day, and He even knows what you're thinking. (Crazy, right?)

When you realize that your Master Artist, the One who designed you, knows every single thing about you, does it calm you down? He's got everything under control! Those issues you're facing at school, that relationship you're struggling with, that fight you had with your mom—He knows. He cares. And He's already working on it.

You can trust Him, girl. Even before you speak a word, He's taking care of the things that matter to you.

Lord, I'm so glad You know me. (Hey, I do my best not to let others know the hidden details of my life, but I can't hide anything from You!) Thanks for caring. Amen.

HE LIVES THROUGH YOU

I have been crucified with Christ. It is no longer I who live,
but Christ who lives in me. And the life I now live in the flesh I live
by faith in the Son of God, who loved me and gave himself for me.
GALATIANS 2:20 ESV

Jesus lives inside of you.

Wow. Stop to think about that for a moment. If you had no value, if you weren't "worth it" to Him, then why would He choose you to live inside? It's humbling, isn't it? The Almighty Author of all chose you—yes, *you*—to dwell in. Your heart was perfect for His residence. Your thoughts were just the place He wanted to dwell. So He came to stay!

Here's the truth, sweet girl: He adores you. He picks you again and again. And He truly lives inside of you, wanting nothing more than to be with you twenty-four seven.

Jesus did so much for you. He died on the cross and rose again. And He asks that you lay down your selfish desires and live for Him—fully and completely.

He gave. And He wants you to give too.

You gave all, Jesus. You thought I was worth it. I give You my heart, my attitude, and my desires. Thank You for teaching me how to live. Amen.

EVERY HAIR ON YOUR HEAD

"Are not five sparrows sold for two pennies? And not one of them is forgotten before God. Why, even the hairs of your head are all numbered. Fear not; you are of more value than many sparrows".
Luke 12:6–7 esv

God knows how many hairs are on your head right now. (He even knows how many are in your hairbrush or caught in the drain of your bathtub!) If you lost one single, solitary strand of hair, your heavenly Father would know it. That's how deeply He knows you. That's how much He cares.

Your heavenly Father knows the details. If He knows how many hairs you have, do you really think you can hide your broken heart from Him? If He sees the missing strands of hair in the drainpipe, do you think you can hide that "secret" sin from Him? He's got supernatural, bionic, X-ray vision. He sees all. He knows all. And He cares about it all.

So stop hiding! Bring everything into the light, girl. He already knows, anyway.

I won't try to hide anything from You, Lord. You care so much about me. Thanks for thinking I am worth it. Amen.

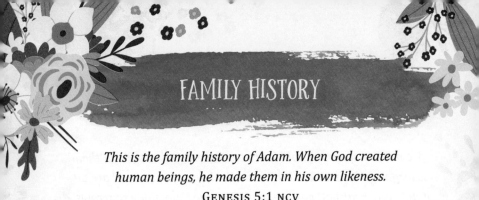

FAMILY HISTORY

This is the family history of Adam. When God created human beings, he made them in his own likeness.
GENESIS 5:1 NCV

Have you ever pulled out the family photo albums and looked at all of the pictures inside? No doubt you were stunned to see how much you look like your grandmother. Or your great-aunt. Or even how much you look like your mom when she was your age.

Family resemblances get passed down from generation to generation. But here's a cool thought—godly resemblances have been carried down from the time of Adam until now.

Think about it this way: God created Adam and Eve in His image. They messed up and were tossed out of the Garden of Eden, but that didn't stop their family from going on. . .and on. . .and on. You're part of that original family, believe it or not. And, like Adam, you were created in God's likeness. Isn't it cool to think that some of Adam's and Eve's DNA lives in you too? Even more exciting, if you could see a photo of your heavenly Father, you might just think, *Wow, I can definitely see the family resemblance!*

I love being part of Your big family, Lord!
Thanks for including me. Amen.

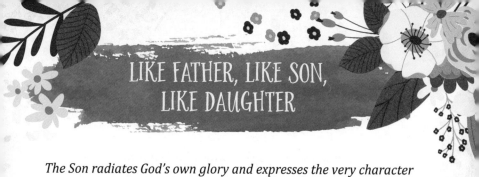

LIKE FATHER, LIKE SON, LIKE DAUGHTER

The Son radiates God's own glory and expresses the very character of God, and he sustains everything by the mighty power of his command. When he had cleansed us from our sins, he sat down in the place of honor at the right hand of the majestic God in heaven.
HEBREWS 1:3 NLT

Jesus is the Son of God. But check out what this verse says about the Son. If you read this verse carefully, you'll see one very important fact: Jesus is a lot like His Dad! Like Father, like Son. And now that you've accepted Jesus as your Savior (you have, haven't you?), you're a lot like Him too!

So what can a daughter or son of God expect to have? Look at the list: the character of God, power, cleansing (a clean heart), and a special place in heaven.

Like Father, like Son, like daughter. And one day you'll all be together for all eternity. God must really think you're something special to include you in all of that!

Sounds like we've got a lot in common, Lord! I can't wait to meet you face-to-face. Amen.

CREATED TO BE CHANGEABLE

*Let the Spirit change your way of thinking and make
you into a new person. You were created to be like God,
and so you must please him and be truly holy.*
EPHESIANS 4:23–24 CEV

In the previous devotions, you've discovered that you were created in the image and likeness of God. You're worthy, not because of anything you've done, but because you've got His DNA. You're His daughter, adored by Him.

But that doesn't mean everything about you is practically perfect in every way. There are still areas of your heart and life that you need to work on, girl! (C'mon, you know it's true!)

Here's some amazing news: the Holy Spirit lives inside you, and He can change your way of thinking and make you a new person. No matter what you've done in the past, He can make all things new. He can set you on a new path. This is one way that you prove you're a daughter of the King—you act like one. Why? Because you love Him!

*I want to please You, Lord! Thanks for giving me
the Holy Spirit so that I can make changes in
my life, to be more holy like You. Amen.*

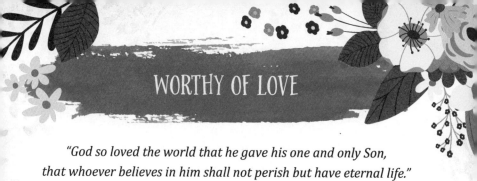

WORTHY OF LOVE

"God so loved the world that he gave his one and only Son,
that whoever believes in him shall not perish but have eternal life."
JOHN 3:16 NIV

God gave His Son so that you could have eternal life.

Stop to think that through. God didn't have to send His Son. And Jesus didn't have to follow through and come to earth to die for you. But, out of a great love for you, that's exactly what God and Jesus did.

God decided you were worth it. His love was so strong that He gave . . .and gave. . .and then gave some more.

How do you feel when you think about how deep, how wide, how long, and how high the Lord's love is? Does it boggle your mind? Here's some great news: He loves the people you love. Your parents, siblings, friends, even your enemies. He loves mankind with a passion that drove Him all the way to the cross. And He did it all so that you could live with Him forever in heaven one day. (That's a lot of love!)

Thank You, thank You for your sacrifice on the cross,
Jesus! You thought I was worth dying for. Wow! Amen.

HE CALLS YOU HIS KID

See what great love the Father has for us that He
would call us His children. And that is what we are.
For this reason the people of the world do not know
who we are because they did not know Him.

1 JOHN 3:1 NLV

Have you ever met a dad who loved to talk about his kids? Maybe he pulled out pictures and showed off each one, telling story after story. Talk about a proud papa!

God's a lot like that dad when it comes to His kids. He's got a lot of great stories to tell. He's also got your picture printed on His heart. He loves using the words "My kid" when He talks about you too.

Don't believe it? Check out today's verse! It's because He loves us that God calls us His kids. And the reason that you don't always fit in in this world? The reason people don't get it? It's because they don't "get" Him. If they truly knew the Dad, they would understand the kids.

Don't get offended if friends don't understand your relationship with God. Just keep praying for them, that they can come to know Him too.

You call me Your kid, Lord! You must love me a lot! Amen.

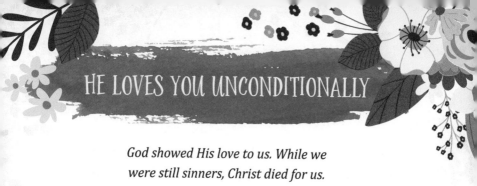

HE LOVES YOU UNCONDITIONALLY

God showed His love to us. While we
were still sinners, Christ died for us.
ROMANS 5:8 NLV

Imagine you got a new puppy. He was absolutely adorable. So cute! You adored every single thing about him. . .until he peed on the rug. And ate the computer cord. And chomped on your expensive tennis shoes. And left a "surprise package" under the bed. Ugh! Your feelings really changed when months went by and he still refused to cooperate. Did you make a mistake in adopting him?

Here's the deal: the things (and people) we love are easier to love when they behave. When they're naughty, not so much. (That's called "conditional" love; we love them under certain conditions.)

God's love toward you is unconditional. It doesn't rely on your behavior. He doesn't look at you on the "naughty" days and say, "Ugh! I wish I'd never adopted this one!" Instead, He embraces you, whispers, *"You can do better"* in your ear, and then encourages you with His love.

While we were yet sinners, Christ died for us. And He'd do it all over again too!

Jesus, thank You for seeing past my sin. Show me how
to have unconditional love toward others like You do! Amen.

27

HE SINGS OVER YOU!

"The Lord your God is with you, a Powerful One Who wins the battle. He will have much joy over you. With His love He will give you new life. He will have joy over you with loud singing."
ZEPHANIAH 3:17 NLV

God loves to throw a good party. No, really! He gets so giddy when He looks at you that He bursts into song. He's like that new mother who sings lullabies to her baby. He's also like the guy from that over-the-top musical you saw, the one who spontaneously burst into song for no obvious reason. That's how crazy He is about you, girl.

Maybe you didn't realize how strongly God feels about you. Maybe you look at your life—your looks, your actions, your lack of talent—and wonder how anyone could possibly celebrate you, of all people.

It's time to realize your worth! The Creator of the universe thinks you're so special that He's writing chart-topping songs just for you. Can you hear them? Lean in close! He might be singing one at this very moment.

Lord, You really love me that much? You're seriously bursting into song? Over me? Wow! Thank You for finding value in me. I can't wait to hear what You're about to sing next. Amen.

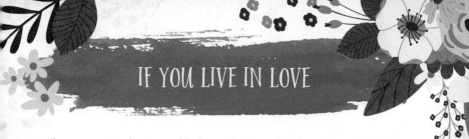

IF YOU LIVE IN LOVE

We have come to know and believe the love God has for us. God is love.
If you live in love, you live by the help of God and God lives in you.
1 JOHN 4:16 NLV

People annoy you. They get on your nerves. Some of them you'd love to write off. *Sayonara!* So long, folks!

Only, you can't. They're your brothers. Sisters. Parents. Friends. They're your teachers. Mentors. Pastors.

So you take a deep breath and try to see their value, the same way Jesus finds value in you. You wonder, *How? How do I do that?* And then you read a verse like the one above from 1 John 4:16 and the answer becomes glaringly obvious: "If you live in love, you live by the help of God." Ouch. So if you just act more like God, then you'll receive His help to get through the challenges? Sounds about right.

Who are you struggling with most? Ask for the Lord's supernatural love to penetrate your heart for that person. If you offer love, you might just be surprised to see how quickly God rushes in and provides the help you need to get past what you're feeling.

I want to learn to live in love, Jesus.
Help me. Please?! Amen.

GIVE UP, GIRL!

We have power over all these things through Jesus Who loves us so much. For I know that nothing can keep us from the love of God. Death cannot! Life cannot! Angels cannot! Leaders cannot! Any other power cannot! Hard things now or in the future cannot! The world above or the world below cannot! Any other living thing cannot keep us away from the love of God which is ours through Christ Jesus our Lord.
ROMANS 8:37–39 NLV

You can try all day, but nothing you ever do will drive God away. Even your worst behavior. (Think of that time you slammed your bedroom door in your mom's face.) Even when you say something truly hateful. (Think of that time you told your kid sister you wish she'd never been born.) Even then, Jesus still adores you. He still finds value in you and thinks you're worthy of love.

Nothing that happens in this lifetime can separate you from the love of Jesus. He's not going anywhere. Sure, you might feel like He's a million light-years away, but the one who's pulling back is you, not Him.

Give up, girl. You're His. He's yours. Ain't nothing gonna change that.

I give up, Jesus! You've chased me down with Your love. Thank You for thinking I was worth the chase. Amen.

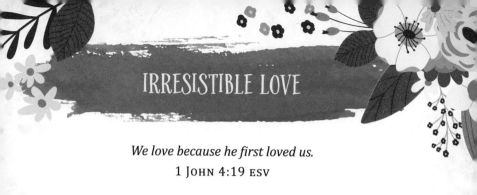

IRRESISTIBLE LOVE

We love because he first loved us.
1 John 4:19 esv

Have you ever wondered how certain couples end up together? Maybe he's super handsome and she's just so-so. Or maybe she's a real beauty queen, young and beautiful, and he's older and wrinkled. How in the world did they choose each other?

Love is fascinating, isn't it? You never know who you're going to fall head over heels in love with. But one thing is for sure—some people make themselves irresistible! They win you over with their kindness, their authentic love and grace. You simply can't turn them away.

Think about that friend who was once a stranger. She wasn't your type. Not in your "usual" friend group. But her kindness won you over. After a while you couldn't think of any logical excuses why you shouldn't accept her friendship. Now you're BFFs.

She learned from the Master! Jesus is the King of loving first. He won't stop until He's won you over. Just like that friend, His love is irresistible.

You didn't give up on me, Jesus! You just kept loving and loving and loving. You must really think I'm worth it! I don't get it, but I'm super grateful. Amen.

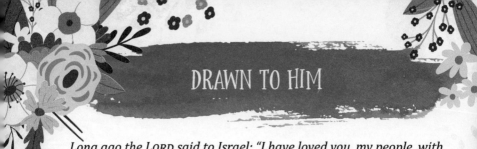

DRAWN TO HIM

Long ago the LORD said to Israel: "I have loved you, my people, with an everlasting love. With unfailing love I have drawn you to myself."
JEREMIAH 31:3 NLT

Let's face it: we're drawn to certain people. Oh sure, some are popular and magnetic, but then there are others. That quiet girl in your science class. That boy who sits alone in the lunchroom. That woman who walks her dog past your house every day. You can't put your finger on why, but you're drawn to them.

Here's a deep, life-changing truth: God's Spirit woos you. Even now, He's saying, *"Be nice to this one!"* or *"Include that one!"* Why? Because He adores them. And He also knows that you need good people in your world, ones who will love and accept you for who you are. (Not just everyone will do that, after all.)

Include. Don't exclude. Love. Demonstrate His unfailing love in all you do.

Thanks for pointing out certain people to me, Jesus. Nothing breaks my heart more than knowing some of them don't feel included. May I have a heart to love as You love. May they be drawn to me as I am drawn to You. Amen.

THANKFUL FOR LOVE

Give thanks to the God of heaven,
for his steadfast love endures forever.
PSALM 136:26 ESV

God's love is steadfast. It's not fluctuating. (Hey, it's not like the weather—hot one day, cold the next. He's got boiling-hot love for you every day of the week!)

So how do you feel about that? When you ponder His steadfast love, is your heart overwhelmed? (Hint: It should be!) If so, take the time to thank Him. Spend a few minutes in prayer saying things like, "Jesus, I don't get it, but I'm so grateful!" When you come to Him with a heart filled with praise, guess what your supernatural Savior does? If you said, "Pours out even more love!" you would be right. He keeps that waterfall coming.

Now here's the tricky part: He wants you to share steadfast love with others. Not just with a few but with all the people in your circle of influence—at school, in your neighborhood, everywhere!

Before your heart hits the floor, remember: No pressure, girl! Ask for His help, and He will love them through you.

I'm going to need Your help to love others as You love me, Jesus, but I'm willing to give it a try! Amen.

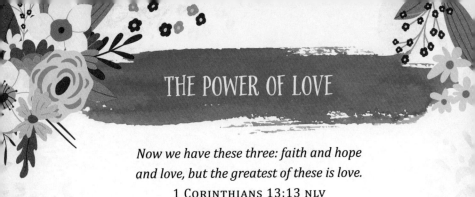

THE POWER OF LOVE

*Now we have these three: faith and hope
and love, but the greatest of these is love.*
1 CORINTHIANS 13:13 NLV

It's the greatest force on planet earth, with more potential than a nuclear power plant. More life changing than an atomic bomb. More hopeful than any peace treaty between nations.

Love is the force that propelled God to send His Son, Jesus, to the earth. Love was what propelled Jesus to accept the invitation to die for us. And love lives and breathes in the person of the Holy Spirit, who came to live inside of you when you accepted Jesus as your Savior. (You have done that, haven't you?)

Love can change anything. Literally, *anything*. It can mend a broken relationship, fix a busted heart, even change the outcome of nations at war. This force is so powerful that the enemy of your soul (that slippery devil) works overtime to keep people from caring about one another. He knows the power of love. But you're on to him! Through the love of God, you've discovered your worth, found the courage to love others, and seen hope for mankind.

Oh, the power of Your love, God! It blows me away! Amen.

SHOW IT, DON'T JUST FEEL IT

God showed how much he loved us by sending his only Son into this wicked world to bring to us eternal life through his death. In this act we see what real love is: it is not our love for God but his love for us when he sent his Son to satisfy God's anger against our sins. Dear friends, since God loved us as much as that, we surely ought to love each other too.
1 John 4:9–11 tlb

There are so many different ways to show love. Some people show it by giving quality time. Others love to do stuff for those they love, like washing the dishes, cleaning the house, and so on. Still others offer words of affirmation: "I'm so grateful for you." "I'm glad God brought you into my life." "Wow, you're really good at that. You're so talented!"

You get the point. No matter how you show love to the people in your circle, it's important to show it. It's not enough just to feel it. God shows you, after all! His Word is filled with words of affirmation, and He's proven that quality time is His thing! (He loves hanging out with you.)

Don't just feel it; show it. Every day, in every way. When you live like this, people actually believe that they have worth.

Thanks for the nudge, Jesus! I need to show it, not just feel it. Amen.

A COVENANT OF LOVE

"The mountains may move and the hills disappear, but even then my faithful love for you will remain. My covenant of blessing will never be broken," says the LORD, *who has mercy on you.*
ISAIAH 54:10 NLT

Have you ever made a covenant with someone? What's a covenant, you ask? It's more than a promise. It's a pledge, a commitment. Maybe you committed to do something for your teacher. Or maybe you covenanted with a friend that you would stick with her, even if everyone else walked away.

God takes covenants very seriously. In the Old Testament days, He "sealed the deal" (made the promise public) with the shedding of animal blood. Priests would offer sacrifices in the temple. In the New Testament, we see the ultimate bloodshed when Jesus went to the cross as the final sacrifice for us all.

God could have chosen a different way, but He opted to covenant with you, girl. And He wants you to know that He's covenanted His love for you. You were worth it to Him. Worth the trip to the cross. Worth the pain of the death of His Son. And worth the mercy He continues to pour out, even now.

I'm so grateful for Your love covenant, Lord!
Thank You for thinking I am worth it. Amen.

WHEN THINGS GET AWKWARD

Your unfailing love is better than life itself; how I praise you!
PSALM 63:3 NLT

You tried to fix the broken friendship, but you failed. Nothing you did worked. Not that I'M SO SORRY! text. Not that LET'S JUST MEET AND TALK THIS OUT suggestion. Or that I TOTALLY MESSED THIS UP, PLEASE FORGIVE ME! note you sent. The relationship is now a thing of the past. You've parted ways. You don't speak. Things are. . .awkward. You keep thinking this is a hurdle your friend has to jump, that she will eventually come to her senses, but she doesn't.

Now think about your relationship with God. Can you ever picture a time when He will shun you like that friend did? It's impossible. It goes against the nature and character of God to shut you out, to walk away, to let things get awkward.

Girl, if things between you and God ever feel out of sorts, consider this hard truth: it's probably you, not Him. In fact, it's definitely you!

His love is unfailing. Even in the hardest of times, He will fight for a relationship with you. Why? Because He thinks you're totally worth it.

Thank You for not giving up on me, Lord. I don't ever want things to get awkward between us. Amen.

YOUR MASTER GARDENER

GOD's loyal love couldn't have run out, his merciful love couldn't have dried up. They're created new every morning. How great your faithfulness! I'm sticking with GOD (I say it over and over). He's all I've got left.

LAMENTATIONS 3:22–24 MSG

You glance out at the garden and notice the leaves on your mom's favorite plant are turning brown. Ugh. Is that beautiful flower doomed to death? Sure looks like it. Then you check again the next week and notice it's springing back to life. What happened? Did she water it? Add fertilizer?

God is the best gardener of all! He pours out love like early morning dew on the plants in your proverbial garden. Just when you think there's no chance, He waters again. And again. And again. He fertilizes with His mercy, His grace, His peace. And before long, you're springing to life just like that flower.

No wonder you're so in love with Him now! You've figured out that He finds you so loveable, so precious, that He won't quit, no matter what. He'll go to any lengths to prove His love for you.

Thank You for being the Master Gardener, Lord! I won't wither as long as You take care of my heart. Amen.

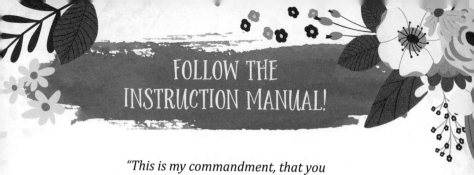

FOLLOW THE INSTRUCTION MANUAL!

"This is my commandment, that you love one another as I have loved you."
JOHN 15:12 ESV

Imagine the fuel pump went out on your dad's car. Instead of taking it to the shop, he looked at you and said, "Okay, girl. Roll up your sleeves. We're going to get this thing fixed, just the two of us."

After taking a moment to panic, you'd probably do what? Hop online and search for specifics about his particular car model. You'd study, study, study and then use what you'd learned to help him replace that fuel pump.

When it comes to the "How do I love others?" question, the answer is the same. Study the instruction manual. Crack open that Bible. Read those verses about love. Forgiveness. Grace. Mercy. Study, study, study. . . and then apply what you've learned. You might not get the problem fixed right away, but if you keep working on it, keep studying, keep applying your newfound knowledge, you'll make huge progress. And who knows, you might even turn out to be an expert!

Thanks for the reminder that answers are found in Your Word, Lord. I'll study and do things Your way! Amen.

DO YOUR PART

By putting our trust in God, He has given us His loving-favor and has received us. We are happy for the hope we have of sharing the shining-greatness of God. We are glad for our troubles also. We know that troubles help us learn not to give up. When we have learned not to give up, it shows we have stood the test. When we have stood the test, it gives us hope.

ROMANS 5:2–4 NLV

"Insert your debit card, please," the clerk says. So you do. You stick it in the slot and the transaction goes through. But what if you refused to put the card into the slot? Would you still receive the item? No way!

The same is true when you choose to put your trust in God. In some ways, it's like sticking that debit card into the slot. In goes your trust, out comes His loving favor and hope. In goes your obedience, out comes His shining greatness.

Doing what He asks you to do is the key that unlocks nearly every door. Life will give you a zillion tests. You'll want to do things your way. But every time, your heavenly Father will ask you to insert your trust in Him. When you do, He'll always come through for you. You mean that much to Him.

I get it, Lord! I do my part, You do Yours.
Thanks for caring so much. Amen.

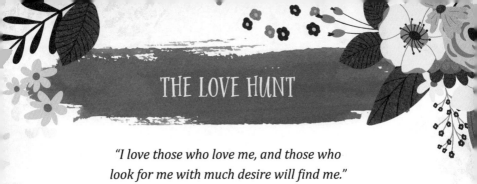

THE LOVE HUNT

*"I love those who love me, and those who
look for me with much desire will find me."*
PROVERBS 8:17 NLV

You've lost your keys. *Again.* You search your purse, your backpack, your bedroom. You look in the laundry room, even check the dryer vent. (Hey, stranger things have happened!) But those keys don't turn up until your mom happens to find them in the refrigerator next to the chocolate cake. Oops.

That might seem like a silly example, but God wants you to treat love like you treat those missing keys. Hunt it down. Don't give up until you find it. Those unkind people you meet along the way? They're like the dryer vent—closed off and hot natured. But look there anyway. The complicated ones? They're like your backpack, overfilled with too much stuff. But look there anyway. Some are easy and sweet, like that chocolate cake. They're easy to love, so you gravitate toward them. But don't overlook the others, girl!

You'll find love every single place you look. You really will. So don't give up. It's one hunt that's worth it in the end!

*Thanks for the reminder to stay on the love hunt, Jesus.
I won't give up. After all, You've never given up on me! Amen.*

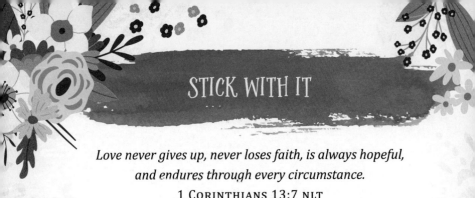

STICK WITH IT

Love never gives up, never loses faith, is always hopeful,
and endures through every circumstance.
1 CORINTHIANS 13:7 NLT

You want to give up. It's too hard. That chemistry test you just took? Yeah, you bombed it. Oh, not because you didn't study. You *did* study. You just don't get it. You've tried and tried and tried. Is it too late to drop the class? Could you take computer lab instead?

This is just one of many, many times you'll be tempted to give up, sweet girl. But if you stick with it and if you learn the material, you'll be so proud of yourself in the end! And, in many ways, this is a test—but not the kind you take in school. It's a life test. If you can pass this life test, you'll learn a valuable lesson: Persistence pays off.

It pays off in relationships too. With those tough cases, especially! Don't give up on yourself and don't give up on others. Keep loving. Keep hoping. Keep trying.

Lord, I feel like a quitter sometimes. I want to stop, to throw my hands up in the air and say, "Enough already!" But You're showing me that some things (and all people) are totally worth the effort. Amen.

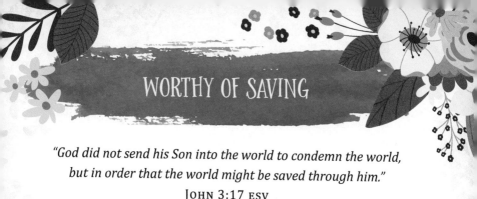

WORTHY OF SAVING

*"God did not send his Son into the world to condemn the world,
but in order that the world might be saved through him."*
JOHN 3:17 ESV

Jesus came to earth to save mankind from sin and death. You've already figured out that He did it out of love—for you and for all of His kids. He did it because He felt you were worth it.

Now look at the second part of that promise. He didn't do it to make you feel bad. There's enough shame and blame going around already. God didn't sent Jesus to point fingers or inflict guilt but to save mankind once and for all—without condemnation. He's like that lifeguard diving into the pool at just the right moment to save the child from drowning. If He hadn't taken the plunge, we would've gone under. And there would've been no rescue after that. (Also, no lifeguard ever tries to make the person he rescued feel guilty after he's saved them!)

Wow! What a Savior. He took the deep dive, and all for us! Don't feel bad about it, girl. Celebrate that free gift today.

*Jesus, thank You! I'm sorry about my sin, but I'm
so glad You're not holding it against me. Amen.*

NOT YOUR OWN DOING

By grace you have been saved through faith.
And this is not your own doing; it is the gift of God.
EPHESIANS 2:8 ESV

Not just anyone could have saved humanity. Think about that for a moment. Even if you had come up with the idea to die on a cross, offering your life in place of others', it wouldn't have worked. Why? Because only God can offer grace and forgiveness. Humans can't. Angels can't. Nothing in creation can.

Salvation had to come through One who was perfect. (And let's face it, girl. . .you're not perfect.) How could an imperfect person carry the sins of someone else? His own sins would be weighty enough.

But Jesus never sinned. Not even once. Oh, He had plenty of opportunities, but He didn't blow them. He lived a sinless life, and because of that sinless state, He was qualified to offer Himself as a sacrifice.

Wow! That's a lot to take in, right? Your sinless Savior cared enough about you that He went to the cross to carry the weight of your sins. What a gift!

I could never have done it, Jesus!
Only You are perfect! Amen.

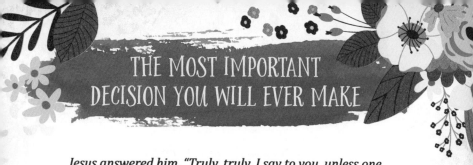

THE MOST IMPORTANT DECISION YOU WILL EVER MAKE

Jesus answered him, "Truly, truly, I say to you, unless one is born again he cannot see the kingdom of God."
JOHN 3:3 ESV

You'll make a *l-o-t* of important decisions in your life. Who you'll date (and eventually marry). Where you'll go to college. What you'll study. What sort of occupation you'll have. How many children you'll have. Where you'll live. What friends you'll keep in your inner circle.

On and on the list goes. And you get to choose all of that! No one is forcing you, one way or the other.

Of all the decisions you'll make in this lifetime, there's one that trumps the others: Will you choose to follow Jesus Christ? If you make the right decision and accept Jesus as Lord of your life, then all of those other decisions will be easier. Why? Because the Holy Spirit will be living inside of you and can help you discern the best path.

If you haven't already done so, pray this simple prayer:

Jesus, thank You for dying on the cross! Come and live in my heart. Be my Lord and Savior. I give myself to You, wholly and completely. I'm Your child, now and forever. Amen.

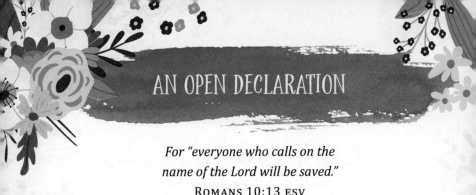

AN OPEN DECLARATION

*For "everyone who calls on the
name of the Lord will be saved."*
ROMANS 10:13 ESV

Why do you suppose God is so keen on you making an open declaration of your faith in Him? Why not just keep it hidden in your heart?

Here's a cool nugget of truth: the Lord wants to use you. Yes, *you*. He didn't just choose you to be saved, to live forever with Him; He also wants you to realize that you have the potential to lead others to Him.

He thinks you're amazing! But He thinks the rest of mankind is pretty amazing too. And someone has to tell them about what Jesus did on the cross. If not you, then who?

It's simple math, really. Think of it this way: if every Christian led just one other person to the Lord, then the number of Christians on the planet would double. Whoa!

God picked you. So don't keep your faith to yourself, girl! Declare it—openly!

I'll share the news of what You've done, Jesus! Thanks for saving me. And thanks for using me to reach others. Amen.

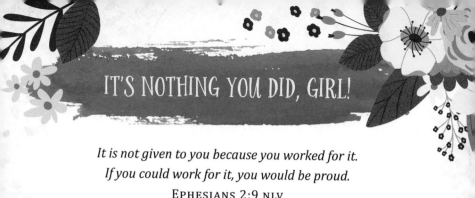

IT'S NOTHING YOU DID, GIRL!

It is not given to you because you worked for it.
If you could work for it, you would be proud.
EPHESIANS 2:9 NLV

You love those pats on the back, don't you? They can make you feel so good. Some people work really hard but never get the encouragement they need from others. That's a tough way to live.

No matter how hard you work, no matter how many good deeds you do, you can't save yourself. You could give money to the poor, travel to developing countries, feed the homeless, and even take care of the sick, and it wouldn't earn you a ticket to heaven. There's only one way to get there, and that's through the sacrifice of Jesus on the cross.

Does this mean God doesn't want you to do good deeds? Oh, He definitely wants you to live this way. Good deeds are. . .well, good! Even though they don't save you, they shine a light on God, which is a wonderful thing!

Jesus thought you were worthy enough to save. And He would do it again too!

I get it, Lord. I didn't earn it. But that doesn't mean I can live any way I like. So I'll live for You! Amen.

ONLY THROUGH JESUS

Jesus said to him, "I am the way, and the truth, and the life. No one comes to the Father except through me."

JOHN 14:6 ESV

Some people say there are many roads to heaven. They think that Muhammad will lead them there. And Buddha. And Krishna. And a host of others. But if you read the Bible closely, you'll learn a very important truth: there's only one way, and it's through Jesus Christ. He's not ready to share the spotlight with anyone else, and for good reason! He's the One True God! (If you were the original, would you want to share the limelight with counterfeits?)

Why do you suppose God has a Jesus-only route to heaven? Could it be that He doesn't want anyone else to take the credit for what He's done? Or could it be that He knows the truth from a lie? Any other god isn't the One True God. The counterfeits fall short by comparison.

Only Jesus is worthy. None other. And in case you're wondering why (or how) He finds you, His daughter, worthy—it's because you are His and His alone.

There's only one ticket to heaven, Jesus, and it's through You! I won't look for any other doors. No counterfeits for me. Amen.

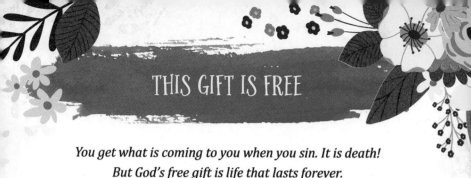

THIS GIFT IS FREE

You get what is coming to you when you sin. It is death!
But God's free gift is life that lasts forever.
It is given to us by our Lord Jesus Christ.
ROMANS 6:23 NLV

Have you ever gotten caught in one of those freebie schemes? You see a product online and it's advertised as being 100 percent free. Only, when you add it to your cart, there's a $19.95 shipping fee. Or maybe you get ready to download a "free" app on your phone only to discover there's a catch. You only get it free for seven days, and then you'll be charged $9.99 a month. Ugh. You're not falling for that trap!

When it comes to free gifts, there's one that really is completely and totally free, and that's the gift of salvation. You don't have to pay for it. Jesus already paid. There's no catch. It's really His gift for you. Of course, you have to receive this gift, in much the same way you'd take a birthday present into your hands and open it. Once you accept that gift from your Savior, it's yours—forever and ever!

Thanks for caring enough about me that You would offer me this precious, free gift, Jesus. I'm so grateful for my salvation. Amen.

YOU AND YOUR HOUSEHOLD

*As he took them outside, he said, "Sirs, what must I do to be
saved?" They said, "Put your trust in the Lord Jesus Christ and
you and your family will be saved from the punishment of sin."
Then Paul spoke the Word of God to him and his family. It was
late at night, but the man who watched the prison took Paul
and Silas in and washed the places on their bodies where they
were hurt. Right then he and his family were baptized.*
ACTS 16:30–33 NLV

Today's verses come at the tail end of another great Bible story. Paul and
Silas had been taken prisoner for their faith. (Can you imagine?) While
in prison, they sang worship songs. At the midnight hour, an earth-
quake hit and the whole prison was shaken! Prisoners were set free
from their chains!

The guard, worried for his life, gave his heart to the Lord. Paul and
Silas went with him to his house, where they shared the Gospel message
with the man's whole family—and they were all saved.

God adores you and thinks you're worthy of saving, but He never
meant for it to be just about you. No, girl. He wants to see your whole
family come to know Him—every last person! So stand in faith and believe!

Thank You for dying for my whole family, Jesus! Amen.

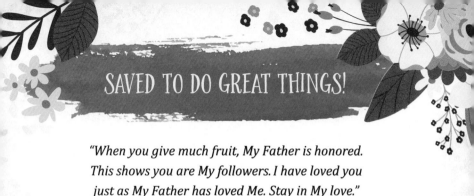

SAVED TO DO GREAT THINGS!

"When you give much fruit, My Father is honored. This shows you are My followers. I have loved you just as My Father has loved Me. Stay in My love."
JOHN 15:8–9 NLV

Why did God choose to save you, His precious child? Because He loves you, sure, but why else? Girl, He's got amazing things in your future. He can see all of the many things you're going to accomplish, and He can't wait to get started! (If you could see, you'd be excited too!)

"What things?" you ask. Oh, if only you could see! One thing's for sure—He's aiming high with you. He sees your value and knows that you're going to make a difference for Him, so brace yourself for some big stuff.

When you "give much fruit," as today's verse says, you are productive. God loves a "fruity" kid. It's better to be productive than to wither on the vine. So stay close to Him. Pray this simple prayer: "Lord, what do You have for me to do?" Then listen for His still, small voice and be ready to step up and follow His lead!

Lord, You saved me so that I could do big things for You. I'm ready! Amen.

HIS SPIRIT IS A GIFT

Peter said to them, "Repent and be baptized every one of you in the name of Jesus Christ for the forgiveness of your sins, and you will receive the gift of the Holy Spirit."
ACTS 2:38 ESV

Imagine it's Christmas morning and you're opening your presents. You've been given something you've always dreamed of—an expensive camera. You can hardly believe your eyes! You love photography. Then, just when you think you've opened the last gift, you realize there's one more. You open a card that reads, "Use your camera on your upcoming trip to Paris."

Whoa. That changes everything! The first gift was light-years beyond anything you'd imagined, but the second? What did you do to deserve that?

That's how it is when you give your heart to Jesus. You get the best gift ever (salvation), and then, just for kicks, God throws in the gift of His Spirit, who comes to live inside of you.

Why would God offer a twofer special, wrapped up in ribbons and bows? Because you're worth it, girl!

God, You have blessed me beyond my wildest dreams. You've given me eternal life and the gift of Your Spirit. I'm blown away! Amen.

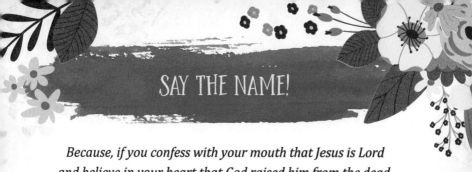

Because, if you confess with your mouth that Jesus is Lord and believe in your heart that God raised him from the dead, you will be saved. For with the heart one believes and is justified, and with the mouth one confesses and is saved.
ROMANS 10:9–10 ESV

There's so much power in the name of Jesus. If only you realized! You would be calling on Him first, in *every* situation.

Picture yourself in the middle of a crisis. Instead of calling a friend or a family member, you cry out one name: Jesus! And in that moment, peace floods your soul.

You were created by Him to want and need Him, not just in crises but on good days too. He wants you to love Him and to recognize the power in His name. He sees value in you, but He wants you to see the full value in Him as well! (Hey, if you had a bodybuilder friend, wouldn't you call on him to protect you if a situation arose?)

Call on Him. Don't wait. Don't pick up the phone and punch in your friend's number. Call Jesus instead. He can do, in an instant, what your friend couldn't do in years of trying. He saved you for relationship, girl!

I call on You today, Jesus. You're the answer to every problem. Your power can fix anything. I'm so blessed to call on You. Amen.

MORE THAN ENOUGH ROOM

"Don't let your hearts be troubled. Trust in God, and trust also in me. There is more than enough room in my Father's home. If this were not so, would I have told you that I am going to prepare a place for you? When everything is ready, I will come and get you, so that you will always be with me where I am."
JOHN 14:1–3 NLT

Remember the story of Mary and Joseph? They got to Bethlehem, and Mary went into labor. They started looking for a place to stay, but the inn was full. "No vacancy." So they ended up in a stable, where baby Jesus was born.

Aren't you glad God never hangs out the NO VACANCY sign? His door is open to you, His child. In fact, you're so valuable to Him that He gives you a key and says, *"Come in anytime, girl!"*

This is one of those free gifts that you received when you gave your heart to Him. Twenty-four seven access is yours. And when you come into His presence, you never have to be afraid. He's never going to greet you with a harsh word. No way! He'll spread His arms wide and say, *"What took you so long, kiddo? I've been waiting on you!"*

Lord, I won't wait! I'll come to You with my problems, my joys, my sorrows. I'm so grateful Your doors are always open. Amen.

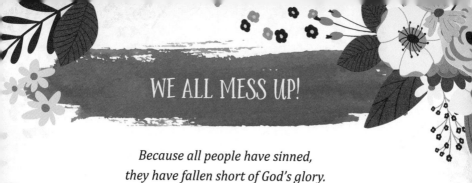

WE ALL MESS UP!

Because all people have sinned,
they have fallen short of God's glory.
ROMANS 3:23 GW

Imagine you were asked to babysit a class full of toddlers. Two-year-olds. Instead of behaving, they were naughty, naughty, naughty! You tried every trick in the book, but they simply wouldn't obey. The tantrums, the kicking, the biting. . .it went on and on. Ugh! You'd get pretty frustrated, right? (Hey, who could blame you?)

Now imagine how God must feel. He went to all of this trouble to send His one and only Son to die for mankind, and often our response is like a room full of toddlers. We demand our own way. We have a "me, myself, and I" mentality. We fight and bicker with others. We throw tantrums when we don't get our way. In short, we're a bunch of brats!

Maybe you wonder if God ever regrets His decision. He doesn't! Oh, it breaks His heart when we disobey or cause trouble, but He would do it all over again. That's how much He adores all of us.

We all fall short. We all sin. But we don't have to stay that way.

Lord, thank You for caring enough to die for us,
even when we're rebellious and naughty! Amen.

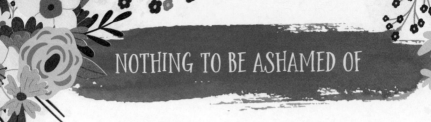

NOTHING TO BE ASHAMED OF

I'm not ashamed of the Good News. It is God's power to save everyone who believes, Jews first and Greeks as well.
ROMANS 1:16 GW

There's an ongoing conversation about which "people group" God loves the most. He first revealed Himself to the Jewish people, and they're pretty high on the list! But then, when Jesus came, the floodgates were open. For the first time, other people had access to the Savior too.

People of every skin color, every nation, every culture, every lifestyle. Jesus died for every single one. And He loves and values every human being exactly the same.

This is one reason we can't be ashamed of the Gospel message. It truly is good news, not just for certain people groups but the whole world. And the whole world needs to hear. Will you tell them? Or will you hide your light under a bushel and pretend it's not important?

Look around you, girl! This world is in chaos. There are signs everywhere that the return of Christ is near. There's no time to waste. He adores you. He saved you. He's given you eternity. Will you share that message with others while you can?

Lord, I won't hesitate! I sense that time is short. I'll share the Gospel with my friends and loved ones so that we can all live in heaven together one day. Amen.

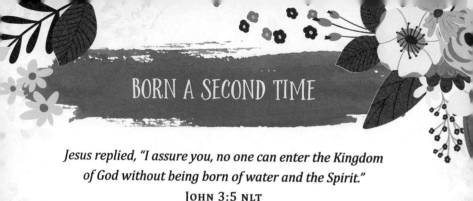

BORN A SECOND TIME

Jesus replied, "I assure you, no one can enter the Kingdom of God without being born of water and the Spirit."
JOHN 3:5 NLT

Maybe today's verse causes you to scratch your head. It's confusing. Was Jesus really saying you have to be born two different times—once in the usual way and then a second time too?

Yep! That's exactly what He was saying. You came into the world the way all babies do. You spent nine cozy months in your mother's womb surrounded by water. Just before birth, that bag of waters broke and out you came! So this verse is right when it says you were born of water.

Then, when Jesus came and offered you eternal life, you were reborn, this time born of His Spirit. Literally, His Spirit came to live inside of you, wiped away your sins, and made you new all over again. This time you were born to live forever. Wow!

Not everyone is born twice, but you are, girl! God must really think a lot of you to give you two different "birth" experiences.

Thank You for making me new all over again, Jesus.
I'm so happy to be born of Your Spirit! Amen.

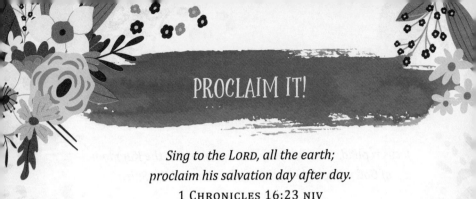

PROCLAIM IT!

Sing to the LORD, all the earth;
proclaim his salvation day after day.
1 CHRONICLES 16:23 NIV

Imagine you received amazing news. Maybe you were accepted into the college of your choice. For years you'd prepared, worked hard, and finally the acceptance letter arrived. No doubt you would flip out (in a good way)! You would text the news to your friends and then hit the airwaves, splashing the celebration across your social media platforms. And why not? Good news is meant to be spread, and the sooner the better!

Why, then, do people hesitate to share the story of how Jesus saved them? Girl, this is better than any cure for any illness. It's a bigger prize than a million-dollar lottery. It's a finer gift than diamonds or jewels. You've been given eternal life from a God who thinks you hung the moon! Why wouldn't you tell others what He's done for you?

Sing to the Lord. Boldly. Proclaim what He's done. Don't worry about who sees or hears. Let the celebration begin!

I won't be intimidated, Lord. I'll shout my story from the rooftops as I sing a song of praise to you! Amen.

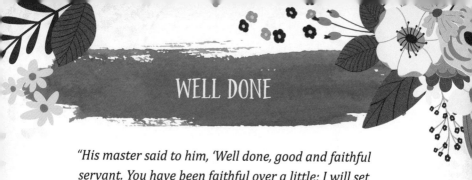

WELL DONE

"His master said to him, 'Well done, good and faithful servant. You have been faithful over a little; I will set you over much. Enter into the joy of your master.'"
MATTHEW 25:21 ESV

Don't you love it when you reach the end of a task and someone says, "Awesome job, girl!" Maybe you've spent the day cleaning your room or organizing your closet. Your mom comes in at the end of it all and gazes around, eyes wide with excitement as she views your work. "Well done!" she exclaims. And she means it.

Let's face it, we could all use a few more "well dones" in our lives. We don't hear them often enough. How exciting, then, to realize that Jesus speaks those words over you on a regular basis. When you bless someone. When you love the unlovable. When you go above and beyond. When you spend time in prayer. When you make good choices. All of these things make His heart happy.

No, you won't earn your way to salvation. He already took care of that on the cross. But when you're faithful in the little, everyday things, He gives you opportunities for bigger things.

So, well done, girl!

Thank You for the encouragement, Lord! And thanks for trusting me with even more to do for You. Amen.

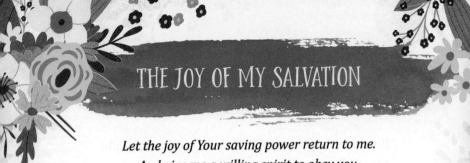

THE JOY OF MY SALVATION

Let the joy of Your saving power return to me.
And give me a willing spirit to obey you.
Psalm 51:12 nlv

Maybe you've heard the expression, "The excitement wore off." That's how it is with Christmas presents. Kids get the things they've begged for. Then time goes by and those gifts are shoved to the back of the closet, forgotten.

The same is true with great news. Maybe your parents have purchased a newer, bigger home. Everything is so exciting at first. You commit to keeping your new room in tip-top shape. But a few months in, it looks like a trash pile—just like the old place.

How easily we forget! We don't keep the celebration going.

When it comes to your salvation, Jesus wants you to keep the party going, girl! Every day can be just as fresh, just as new, just as powerful, as the day you gave your heart to Him. You don't have to lose your joy on the rough days. No way! You're still His child, filled with His Spirit.

Today, if you're struggling, pray the simple prayer below.

Lord, restore the joy of my salvation. May I feel exactly as I felt in that moment when I first came to know You. Amen.

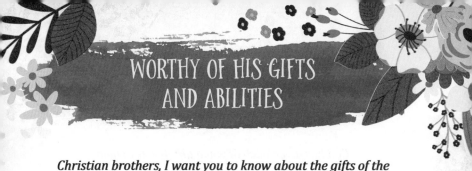

WORTHY OF HIS GIFTS AND ABILITIES

Christian brothers, I want you to know about the gifts of the Holy Spirit. You need to understand the truth about this.
1 CORINTHIANS 12:1 NLV

Imagine you're a parent with a houseful of kids. (This might be a bit of a stretch, but use your imagination!) Now imagine you've got all the money in the world. (Woot!) You can give your kids anything you please. Money. Cars. Houses. Anything.

What would you give them? Would their attitudes help you determine which gifts would go to which child?

Now picture your heavenly Father. He's the owner of, well, everything. He could give you any gifts He likes. But He's choosing based on what's best for you. There are a host of spiritual gifts listed in 1 Corinthians 12: wisdom, teaching, faith, prophecy, miracles, and so on.

There are also artistic and academic gifts. Maybe you're a singer or a dancer or an artist. Maybe you excel at math or writing.

Here's the point: Your Father has unlimited resources, and He values you so much that He wants to lavish His gifts on you. Today, open your hands and heart to receive!

Lord, pour them out! I'll use those gifts for Your glory. Amen.

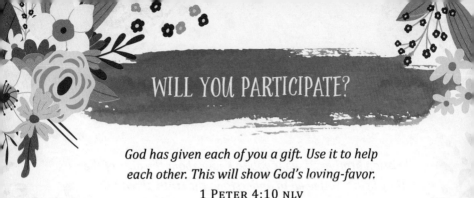

WILL YOU PARTICIPATE?

*God has given each of you a gift. Use it to help
each other. This will show God's loving-favor.*
1 Peter 4:10 nlv

God thinks you're pretty amazing. In fact, He's crazy about you. Because He's crazy about you, He decided to give you lots of gifts—spiritual gifts, academic gifts, artistic gifts, even the gift of gab. (Hey, you love to talk, girl! Admit it!)

Why do you suppose your heavenly Father was so free with those gifts? Why not choose to give you material things, like houses or cars? (Okay, okay. . .He gives those on occasion too.) He chose these other types of gifts because they require something from you. He's looking for active participation from you.

Example: Imagine He gave you the ability to sing, but you never opened your mouth. Imagine He gave you the gift of praying for miracles, but you refused to pray. Imagine He gifted you as a writer, but you never picked up a pen. What would be the point if you did nothing? His gifts require your participation.

And remember, those gifts are meant to be used to help one another. So get out there and share them, girl!

*I'll participate, Jesus! I'll use those gifts
You gave me. I'll develop and share them with
others so that they can know You too. Amen.*

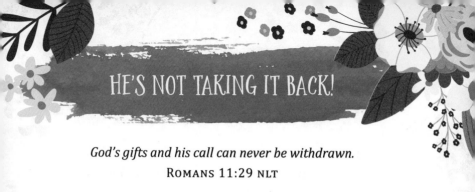

HE'S NOT TAKING IT BACK!

God's gifts and his call can never be withdrawn.
ROMANS 11:29 NLT

Picture yourself at your best friend's birthday party. You've purchased the perfect-for-her gift, something you know she'll love. Sure enough, she opens it and is ecstatic. You hit the nail on the head.

Now picture yourself holding out your hands and saying, "Okay, now that you've seen it, you have to give it back. I never meant for you to keep it." Wait, what? Who does that? No one, and certainly not God!

And yet, some people think He's ready to snatch back the gifts He's given them. They forget today's verse from Romans 11:29. God's gifts can never be withdrawn. If He created you with certain giftings, He means for you to develop and use them. But even if you don't (which is totally up to you), He's not asking for them back. He won't say, "I never meant for you to keep that, girl."

He *does* mean for you to keep that gift. And to grow it into something of beauty. Don't question Him. Don't get caught up in the "Does God really want me to use this gift?" dilemma. He does. So stir it up, girl!

Lord, I guess I'd better keep going, even when I don't feel like it. You're not a quitter, and I won't be either! Amen.

EVERY GIFT IS FROM HIM

Every good gift and every perfect gift is from above,
coming down from the Father of lights, with whom
there is no variation or shadow due to change.

JAMES 1:17 ESV

Some people might look at your musical abilities and say, "Girl, you get that from your mama! She's always been musical too." Or maybe they look at your book smarts and say, "Your grandfather was the same way. He loved math too."

It's true that family traits and propensities can be passed down, but guess who handed out those gifts in the first place? If you said, "God!" you're 100 percent right! Every good and perfect gift comes down from the Father of lights, passed out to those He loves. And isn't it interesting that today's verse uses the phrase "Father of lights" when talking about the gifts He gives His kids? They're meant to be used as a light, to illuminate the pathway for those you meet.

Walk in your gift, and it will make a way for you. It will light your path. It will guide you to where you need to go. The Father of lights will make sure of it, girl!

My gifts are from You, Lord! Thanks for letting them light my way. Amen.

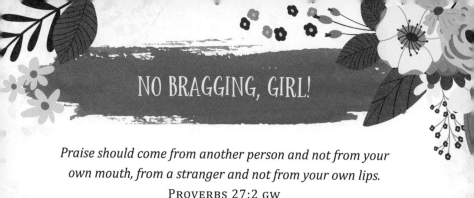

NO BRAGGING, GIRL!

Praise should come from another person and not from your own mouth, from a stranger and not from your own lips.
PROVERBS 27:2 GW

Some people are really talented—and they know it. You know it too. They won't let you forget. There's that one girl. She always gets the solo in choir. And that one boy? He gets the lead in every school play. There's the star quarterback on the football team, the top player on the basketball court, and the girl who always ends up valedictorian. Oh, and the beauty queen. She got the gift of looks!

And then there's you. You're probably not going to rise to the top of the pack, and you're tired of trying. But you're also over the braggers, the ones who sing their own praises.

You've probably figured out by now why God isn't keen on bragging. When you toot your own horn and draw attention to the gifts He gave you, you're pointing a light on yourself, not Him. It's not that He's stingy with His gifts, but He'd like some credit too!

So keep the focus on Him while you're developing those gifts. It's okay to show off a little, but shine the light on Him, not yourself.

Lord, these gifts are from You, meant to bring glory to You, not me. I'll remember that. Amen.

ARE YOU A HAND OR A FOOT?

*As you know, the human body is not made up of only
one part, but of many parts. Suppose a foot says,
"I'm not a hand, so I'm not part of the body!"
Would that mean it's no longer part of the body?*
1 CORINTHIANS 12:14–15 GW

God gave specific gifts to specific people. You might wish you could dance, but you can't. Instead, you're good in science. Or maybe you wish you could stand up in front of a crowd and speak, but your knees knock and your hands shake. You're better off working behind the scenes, in the tech booth. You don't mind not being in the limelight. In fact, you enjoy the backstage stuff.

Get the point? We're all different with unique giftings. It doesn't mean God thinks one person is more special or more deserving than another. He values us all the same! In many ways, we're like a body. You're a foot, she's a hand, he's a mouth, and so on. None of those body parts would be much good without the other, but when everyone works together. . .*wow!* Talk about amazing!

Celebrate the gifts you see in others, girl. They're part of the body too!

*I get it, Lord! No gift is better. No person is better.
We're all loved and gifted by You. Thanks! Amen.*

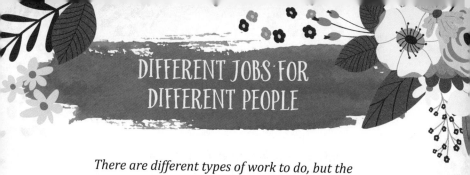

DIFFERENT JOBS FOR DIFFERENT PEOPLE

There are different types of work to do, but the same God produces every gift in every person.
1 Corinthians 12:6 GW

Not everyone is called to be a missionary on a foreign mission field. Not everyone could climb aboard a spaceship and fly to the moon. Not everyone could run an Olympic marathon. And not everyone could stand in front of a third-grade classroom and teach a roomful of kids.

God has different jobs for us to accomplish while we're on this planet. Maybe you'll be a nurse or a doctor. Perhaps you'll be an engineer or a special education teacher. Maybe you'll be a bus driver or own your own restaurant. Whatever you're called by God to do, He's already training and equipping you for that job ahead.

Think about the gifts and abilities He's placed inside of you. They can be used now, sure. But they can be used later on too. Say you're gifted in math or you excel at computer stuff. Can you see how that would serve you well when you're older, if you own your own business?

Different jobs. Different gifts. Same God! He's getting you ready, girl!

I can't wait to see what jobs You have for me in the future, Lord. Thanks for getting me ready! Amen.

YOU CAN TRUST HIS GIFTS

"If your child asks you, his father, for a fish, would you give him a snake instead? Or if your child asks you for an egg, would you give him a scorpion? Even though you're evil, you know how to give good gifts to your children. So how much more will your Father in heaven give the Holy Spirit to those who ask him?"
LUKE 11:11–13 GW

God's gifts are good—not just occasionally, but every single time. Consider the proof found in today's verse. Let's say you asked your dad for a bologna sandwich. Instead, he gave you a bowl full of dead worms. Um. . .no thanks!

Or what if you asked your mom for a slice of the chocolate cake she just baked but she handed you a bar of soap instead? What kind of gift would that be?

You can trust God to give you what you need. If your parents and grandparents know how to give good gifts when you ask, don't you think your heavenly Father does too? He's thinking up exciting gifts, even now. So trust Him! He adores you and wants to lavish you with His absolute best!

I trust You, Lord! You tell me I'm worthy of good gifts, and I'm so grateful for each and every one. Amen.

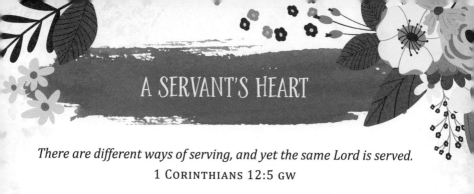

A SERVANT'S HEART

There are different ways of serving, and yet the same Lord is served.
1 CORINTHIANS 12:5 GW

God finds such value in you! If He didn't, He wouldn't waste His time loving you and lavishing you with so many wonderful heavenly abilities. He gets especially excited when He sees that you have a heart for serving others. This is a precious gift. Not everyone handles it well, but when they do. . . wow! People are blessed!

Imagine you were asked to check in on your elderly neighbor's dog while she was at the doctor's office. You did so with a smile on your face, never complaining about how you'd rather be at your friend's house. Instead, you took awesome care of that dog and even baked some cookies for your neighbor while she was away. She came home to a happy dog and a plate full of chocolate chip cookies.

Maybe you never saw your baking skills as a "gift" from God, but in that moment, as you stirred up that batch of yummy delights, it occurred to you: He gave you that ability so that you could serve someone else.

See how fun it is when your gifts are used to bless others?

I get it, Lord! You want me to use my gifts to serve Your people. I'll look for opportunities to do that. Amen.

ASK, SEEK, KNOCK!

"I tell you, ask, and God will give to you. Search, and you will find. Knock, and the door will open for you. Yes, everyone who asks will receive. The one who searches will find. And everyone who knocks will have the door opened."

LUKE 11:9–10 NCV

Ever feel like all of your gifts and abilities have dried up? Maybe you're in a weird season. No one wants to hear you sing. No one wants to see you dance. No one's interested in that latest, greatest book idea you're dreaming up. No one seems interested in the things that get you excited, and you're bummed out.

Just because others don't get it doesn't mean you shouldn't plow forward, girl! Just make sure that you're truly pursuing the right things. Sometimes we chase after dreams just because they sound good in the moment. Not all of those ideas are God ideas. But when they are, keep chasing them! And if opportunities don't present themselves, keep asking, keep seeking, and keep knocking on God's door. If and when the time arises, He'll give you a chance to shine for Him!

Lord, I want to make sure that what I'm doing is truly what You've called me to do. If it is, then give me opportunities, I pray! I'll keep asking, seeking, and knocking until the right doors open. Amen.

70

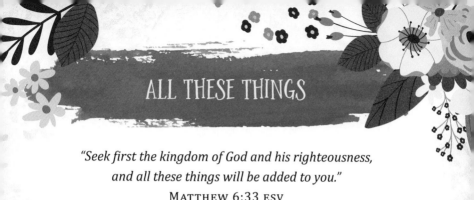

ALL THESE THINGS

"Seek first the kingdom of God and his righteousness, and all these things will be added to you."
Matthew 6:33 esv

Today's verse is interesting, right? If you seek God's kingdom first, then "all these things" will be added to you. What does that mean exactly? And what are "all these things" anyway?

Put God first and then He will give you the desires of your heart. Those things you've been chasing—relationships, opportunities, material possessions, and so on—will only be yours if you chase God instead of chasing them.

Imagine you've got a crush on a great guy. You can't stop thinking about him. But he doesn't seem to notice you. For a while, you can't eat, sleep, or study because he consumes your thoughts. You finally decide to give it a rest. You focus on your relationship with God instead. Then, in God's timing, a door opens for a relationship. Or maybe you're waiting on an opportunity to sing a solo in your youth group's worship team. Instead of pushing the idea on your worship leader, you just focus on Jesus. Then you get a call asking if you will sing.

You get the idea. It's all about putting things in the proper order. Jesus comes first. Everything else falls into place!

I will put You first, Jesus, and You will take care of the rest. Amen.

Whenever you are able, do good to people who need help.
PROVERBS 3:27 NCV

You are a gift to others. It's true! You're a gift to your teacher when you make her job easier. You're a gift to your parents when you obey the first time they ask you to do something. You're a gift to your friends when you take the time to listen. And you're a gift to your church when you work in the nursery or help in kids' church.

There are all sorts of ways you prove what a gift you are, girl! So, as you ponder the many gifts that God pours out to His kids, remember that you're one of them. He's strategic too! He knows how badly that elderly woman next door needs someone to talk to, so He chose you to be a gift to her. He knows that the drama director at school desperately needs someone who's willing to work backstage on the next show, someone who doesn't need to be in the spotlight, so He chose you to be a gift to that teacher.

You're a gift to everyone you help. Keep at it. You're doing great!

Thanks for the reminder that I'm a gift to others, Jesus! Amen.

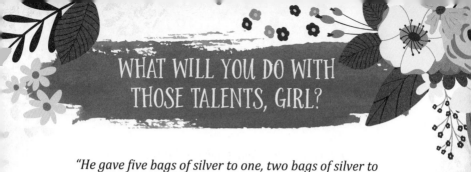

WHAT WILL YOU DO WITH THOSE TALENTS, GIRL?

"He gave five bags of silver to one, two bags of silver to another, and one bag of silver to the last—dividing it in proportion to their abilities. He then left on his trip."
MATTHEW 25:15 NLT

There's a fascinating story in the twenty-fifth chapter of Matthew. A certain master was about to go on a trip. He gave each of his servants money— five bags of silver to one of them, two to another, and one to another. He chose the dollar amounts based on their abilities.

One guy invested the money. Another went to work and doubled the money. One dug a hole in the ground and hid the money. When the master returned and got the financial update, he praised the first two guys but chewed out the third one. Then he gave the first two guys even more responsibilities and opportunities.

That's how it works. God gives you talents and abilities to invest. You either grow them or you don't. Depending on what you do with them, He gives you even more.

This explains why some people really seem to blossom and grow, doesn't it? Could it be that they are wise stewards?

I get it, Jesus! You want me to treat these gifts wisely and cause them to grow. I'll do it, Lord! Amen.

HIS SPIRIT: A LOVELY GIFT

"The Helper, the Holy Spirit, whom the Father will send in my name, he will teach you all things and bring to your remembrance all that I have said to you."

JOHN 14:26 ESV

God gives His kids many, many gifts. Some you can see with your eyes. Some you can hear with your ears. But there's one gift that shows up in a completely different way, and that's the gift of the Holy Spirit.

In the second chapter of Acts, you can read the remarkable story of a remarkable day when the Spirit of God showed up. The disciples were gathered together in an upstairs room, praying and waiting on God. They were pressing in (praying with great anticipation). Then, from out of the blue, the Spirit swept in like flames! And everyone began to speak in other tongues as the Spirit gave them the ability. Wow! What a scene that must've been! They prayed, and God moved!

The Spirit is still moving today—healing hearts, bringing comfort, giving power to the powerless. Miracles are still taking place. The Spirit of God lives inside of every believer, so He's right there, ready to go to work on your behalf. Today, ask for a filling of the Spirit so you have all of the power you could possibly need to do the work God has given you.

Holy Spirit, fill me today, I pray! Amen.

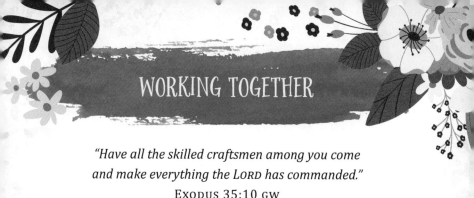

WORKING TOGETHER

"Have all the skilled craftsmen among you come
and make everything the LORD has commanded."
EXODUS 35:10 GW

There's a cool story in the book of Exodus. Moses had been up on the mountain with God. He'd received the Ten Commandments. When he came back down to the people, he shared what he'd learned, then he rallied the troops. He gave them a plan to build a tabernacle, which would become a special place to meet with God (sort of a precursor to our church buildings today).

Each man had a special talent or ability. The iron workers used their skills. The artisans used their skills. The tailors used their sewing skills. And by the time they were all done, the tabernacle was complete.

That's how buildings are made today too. The artisans come together and do their work. What good would walls be without windows? What good would doors be without handles? Every part of the building process relies on the other.

Now you see why God gives so many different gifts. They are meant to work together, girl!

I get it, Lord! My gifts might seem small, but when
I add them to the group, they're huge! Amen.

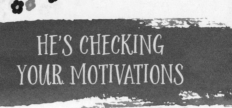

HE'S CHECKING YOUR MOTIVATIONS

So it is with you. Since you are eager for gifts of the Spirit,
try to excel in those that build up the church.
1 CORINTHIANS 14:12 NIV

Oftentimes we want what we want when we want it. We're not thinking of others as we beg God to give us what we've asked for. We're hyper-focused on ourselves.

Maybe you've been there. You've got a certain prize in mind, and you wonder if God will give it to you. Your motivation for wanting it isn't great. You just want it because you want it. No other reason.

God looks at motivations. He adores you, yes; but He wants you to have a pure heart, one bent on serving others, not yourself. *Ouch.* (Hey, the truth hurts!)

Maybe this would be a good day to do a heart check. Do you want what you want when you want it. . .for yourself, or for others? Check your motives, girl! God isn't just after your gifts. He wants your whole heart.

I get it, Lord. I get a little selfish sometimes.
Check my heart. May I become more about
others and less about myself. Amen.

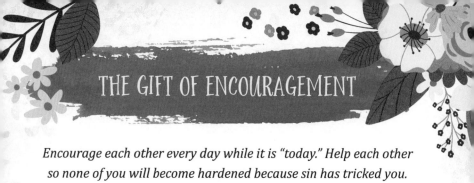

THE GIFT OF ENCOURAGEMENT

Encourage each other every day while it is "today." Help each other
so none of you will become hardened because sin has tricked you.
HEBREWS 3:13 NCV

Are you an encourager? Some girls just have a knack for building others up, for making them feel better when they're down.

Did you ever consider the fact that encouragement might be one of the gifts God has given His kids? It totally is! And He meant for it to be used lavishly, poured out all over the place. Maybe this is why encouragers seem to have a special gift for encouraging others; their abilities come from the Lord. This is why they know just what to say and when to say it. And boy, are they thoughtful! They send cards. They give hugs. They are always there at just the right moment, saying just the right thing to make people feel valuable and loved.

All of these things happen because the Holy Spirit is whispering in their ears: *"Hey, see that one? She needs a card today!"*

Do you want to have the gift of encouragement? Open your eyes, ears, and heart to what's going on around you, then pray that God will use you. He will if you ask!

I want to make others feel better, Lord.
May I be an encourager! Amen.

FAN INTO FLAMES

This is why I remind you to fan into flames the spiritual gift God gave you when I laid my hands on you. For God has not given us a spirit of fear and timidity, but of power, love, and self-discipline.
2 TIMOTHY 1:6–7 NLT

If you're trying to get a campfire going, you'll need to start with a few embers and then fan them into a flame big enough to use as a cook surface. All fires start small but grow, grow, grow!

Now think of the gifts and abilities your heavenly Father has poured into you. Right now, they're tiny embers, barely a spark. But if you "fan them into flames" (work hard to grow them) before long those gifts (like that campfire) will grow!

It takes work. You have to keep that fire lit. Keep practicing. Keep working. Keep studying. Keep doing everything you need to do on your end to develop those gifts. But remember, the ember was placed there by God. You didn't start the fire, He did. So trust Him with it, girl. He's got this!

I'll be disciplined, Lord! You are growing me into a spiritual powerhouse! I won't give up when the fire inside of me feels small. I'll make sure it keeps growing and growing. Amen.

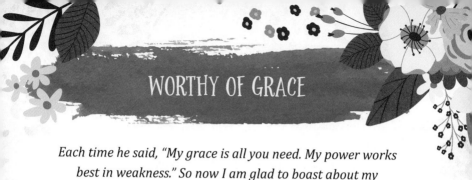

WORTHY OF GRACE

Each time he said, "My grace is all you need. My power works best in weakness." So now I am glad to boast about my weaknesses, so that the power of Christ can work through me.
2 Corinthians 12:9 nlt

Have you ever taken a look at the word *grace*? Some people say it can be broken down into an acronym: GRACE (God's Riches at Christ's Expense). Basically, grace is when God chooses not to give you the punishment you deserve.

Think of it this way: When you were a little kid and you disobeyed, what happened? Maybe you got sent to your room. Or, if the transgression was really bad, you might have been grounded. There were consequences to your actions.

Imagine you did something truly awful—you hurt your brother or called your mom a terrible name. But, instead of punishing you, your mother opted to forgive you. She wrapped you in her arms and said, "I want you to know I still love you." That's grace. Instead of giving you what you deserved (a tongue lashing), you got a quiet, sweet, gentle response.

God is the King of grace speeches. He doesn't want to beat you up. He wants to love you through this. His grace is enough to heal anything!

Thank You for offering grace when I don't deserve it, Jesus!

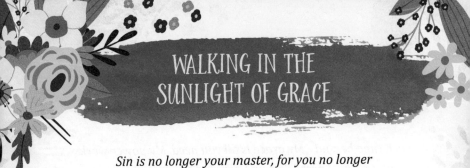

WALKING IN THE SUNLIGHT OF GRACE

Sin is no longer your master, for you no longer
live under the requirements of the law. Instead,
you live under the freedom of God's grace.
ROMANS 6:14 NLT

Imagine you were an inmate in a prison. Every day was the same. You were awakened at a certain time, fed, made to work as a laborer, then sent back to your cell. You rarely saw the sunlight. You lived in the dank, dark prison and followed the rules, day in and day out. Then, one day, the prison doors opened and you were allowed to walk into the sunlight. Wow! What a difference, right?

This might seem like a silly illustration, but that's the difference between living under the law and living under grace. The law served a purpose in its time. And people did their best to live within the confines. But when Jesus died on the cross, He offered a different way, one filled with sunlight. One that depended on Him, not you.

Leave the prison cell of legalism today, girl. Stop beating yourself up for all of the things you've done wrong. Accept God's grace and walk in the sunlight today.

I get it, Lord. I can be bound up (worried about my mistakes) or I can walk in grace. I choose grace! Amen.

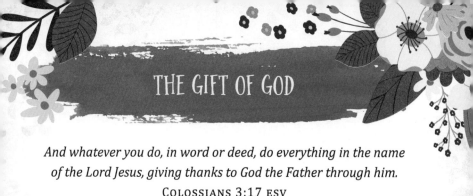

THE GIFT OF GOD

And whatever you do, in word or deed, do everything in the name
of the Lord Jesus, giving thanks to God the Father through him.
COLOSSIANS 3:17 ESV

Imagine you saved a child from drowning in a lake. Several hours later, a newspaper reporter shows up at your house to interview you. You tell the story, and before long, you're a local hero. Everyone knows your name. You can't go anywhere without being recognized.

You start to think a little more about yourself. You start to believe the hype. And you soon become so puffed up no one can stand to be around you.

That's how we human beings are, right? We believe our own press. We give ourselves a lot of credit. But when it comes to saving us, we can't take any of the credit. The One who dove into the lake is Jesus! He pulled you out—a drowning rat—and set your feet on dry ground. His work on the cross accomplished everything necessary for salvation. You didn't do it. Your works didn't do it. And there's no sense in bragging about it, girl. It's all on Him, not you.

I couldn't save myself, but You swept in and saved
the day, Jesus. All of the praise goes to You! Amen.

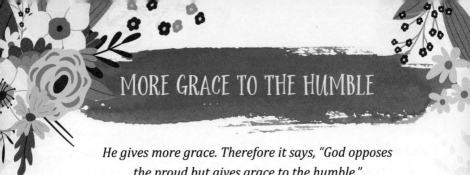

MORE GRACE TO THE HUMBLE

He gives more grace. Therefore it says, "God opposes
the proud but gives grace to the humble."
JAMES 4:6 ESV

"She thinks she hung the moon." Maybe you've heard that expression. (Hopefully no one has said it about you.) When someone thinks they're "all that," it means they've got a big head. They are arrogant, puffed up, hard to be around. To describe a girl like that, some would say, "She's full of herself."

God's not keen on His daughters being full of themselves. On the contrary, He wants you to be full of His Spirit, not yourself! All eyes on Him, not you. That's His way.

Sure, your heavenly Father adores you. He thinks you have incredible value. He feels so strongly about you that He went to the cross to cover your sin. But He doesn't want you to let things go to your head. He prefers you to humble yourself. In fact, today's verse says that He gives grace to the humble. So, if you really want to walk in His favor, turn the spotlight on Him, not you! That's the best way to shine.

Forgive me for the times I've been prideful, Jesus.
I want to shine the light on You, not me. Amen.

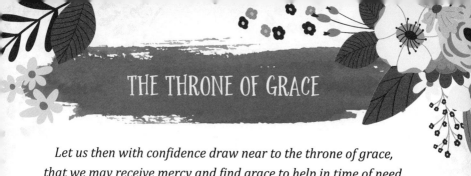

THE THRONE OF GRACE

Let us then with confidence draw near to the throne of grace,
that we may receive mercy and find grace to help in time of need.
HEBREWS 4:16 ESV

Imagine you've been invited to visit the queen of England. You're dressed in your finest, wearing everything you've been instructed. Now it's time to enter the throne room. Your knees are knocking. Your hands are trembling. You're terrified that she will turn you away.

When it comes to approaching Jesus, you can rest easy! Today's verse tells us that we can confidently approach His throne. And look at how the verse describes it: a "throne of grace." Wow! What an image! Instead of a throne of fear, it's a holy, welcoming place where you can expect to find forgiveness, mercy, and love.

God is good. And He adores His kids. He wants nothing but good things for us. So come boldly. No matter what you've done. No matter where you've been. No matter who you've been hanging out with. Just come as you are. Meet Him at His throne of grace today.

I'll come, Jesus. I'm a hot mess. I've done things I shouldn't have. But here I am, ready for some face-to-face grace! Amen.

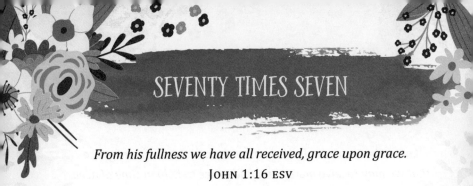

SEVENTY TIMES SEVEN

From his fullness we have all received, grace upon grace.
JOHN 1:16 ESV

Jesus said we are supposed to forgive those who've hurt us—not once, not twice, but seventy times seven. An infinitesimal number of times, we are to offer grace, mercy, and forgiveness. Check it out: Jesus answered, "I tell you, you must forgive him more than seven times. You must forgive him even if he wrongs you seventy times seven" (Matthew 18:22 NCV).

Sounds impossible, doesn't it? And realistically, there are some repeat offenders you need to separate yourself from. Forgive. Offer grace. But scoot to the other side of the room for your psychological well-being!

Here's the point: Jesus offers us grace upon grace. Think of how many times He's forgiven you. Not in your lifetime (that would take too long to calculate). Not over the past year. Not over the past month. Just in the past couple days. How many bad thoughts have you had? How much gossip has escaped your lips? How many people have you bad-mouthed? Yeah, a lot. He offers grace upon grace, so learn from His example, girl. People are worth it.

I get it, Jesus. You offer me
grace. I'll give it to others. Amen.

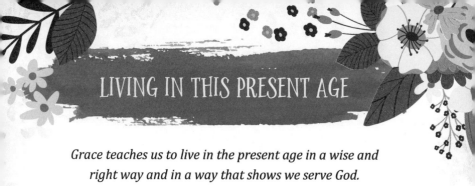

LIVING IN THIS PRESENT AGE

Grace teaches us to live in the present age in a wise and right way and in a way that shows we serve God.
TITUS 2:12 NCV

God placed you in the twenty-first century for a reason. He knew you could handle it. Sure, it's not easy, but you've got everything you need inside of you to make it through these crazy times.

One tool your heavenly Father has placed in your hands, something guaranteed to help, is grace. His grace can (literally) save everyone. Think about it like fertilizer. When you put those nutrients into the ground, the flowers grow. The same is true with grace. When you offer it, even if people don't seem to deserve it, you're really helping the whole garden remain healthy and strong.

People are crazy. This world is off-its-rocker nuts at times. But even with all of the evil surrounding you, offering grace is still the answer. You can live in this present age and still serve God, girl. *Really.* You can.

I don't always feel like I've got what it takes to make a difference, Jesus. Things are crazy. But I will offer grace. Amen.

RIBBONS AND BOWS

And are justified by his grace as a gift,
through the redemption that is in Christ Jesus.
ROMANS 3:24 ESV

You've had a rough day. You're done. *Beyond* done. You don't want to talk about how crummy things are. And the last thing you want to do is to treat others kindly or to offer grace. Don't they see you're at the end of your rope?

Then you look at a verse like this one from Romans 3:24. You see that Jesus kept pouring out grace to you, even on His worst day. As He hung on the cross, as He bled and died, He was thinking of you. His gift of grace was wrapped in ribbons and bows made of blood, sweat, and tears as He agonized on the cross for your sins. And it's through that gift that you have redemption (you've been reborn, redeemed, set free from the past).

When you think about it like that, it's easier to offer grace to others, isn't it? Perspective, girl. It's all about perspective.

What a day that must have been, Jesus! You gave me the greatest gift of all. The least I can do is continue to offer grace, even on the rough days. Amen.

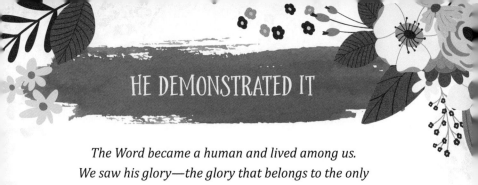

HE DEMONSTRATED IT

The Word became a human and lived among us.
We saw his glory—the glory that belongs to the only
Son of the Father—and he was full of grace and truth.
JOHN 1:14 NCV

"We saw His glory" and "He was full of grace and truth."

Stop to think on those words about your Savior, Jesus Christ. Because He came to earth, because He was fully God and fully man, we were able to catch beautiful glimpses of what grace really looks like.

It looks like Jesus.

It looks like a Savior who stops on the side of the road and heals a lame man. It looks like a teacher who cared enough to provide lunch for five thousand people. It looks like an innocent man who hung on the cross, carrying the sins of people who didn't deserve His love.

That's what grace looks like. And it shines in the eyes of the only One who loved you enough to do all of that because He thinks you're worth it.

The next time you're searching for glimpses of grace, look no further than Jesus.

Oh Jesus! Thank You for showing us what grace and truth look like. We see it in Your eyes. We see it in Your actions. We see it in Your Word. Your love for mankind is immeasurable! What a glorious Savior You are. Amen.

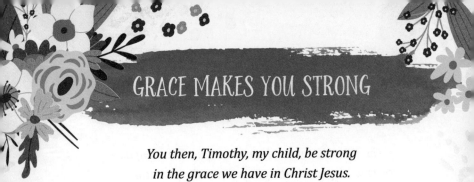

GRACE MAKES YOU STRONG

*You then, Timothy, my child, be strong
in the grace we have in Christ Jesus.*
2 TIMOTHY 2:1 NCV

Some people hear the word *grace* and immediately think of the word *graceful*. To be graceful means you're elegant, flowing, nimble.

Now think of what it takes for a ballet dancer to appear graceful on stage. She might make it look effortless, but that gal is loaded with muscles. She works out every day and whips her body into submission to get it to bend like that. She's stronger than most of us and better capable of withstanding pain. (She would have to be to stand on her toes so long without weeping!)

The same is true when you're a Christian. You might look grace-full on the outside (and you are), but your journey has been tough. It has strengthened you from the inside out. Because you're strong, you can hold your head up high and show others that you've got what it takes to keep going.

You're filled with grace, girl. And it's a grace born of strength!

I've been through some stuff, Jesus! I'm tough on the inside but want to be a reflection of You to everyone I meet. May I reflect grace and truth. Amen.

FOLLOWING AFTER GRACE

The grace of God has appeared, bringing salvation for all people.
TITUS 2:11 ESV

Remember the story of the Pied Piper? He went through town playing his flute, and children followed behind him, mesmerized by the sound. He drew them in, almost hypnotically.

That's kind of how grace is. When you meet someone who's full of grace, you want to latch on to them. (Hey, those folks are pretty rare these days!) You want to follow in their footsteps. Learn from them. Borrow their mannerisms.

When Jesus came to the earth, grace showed up in a big way. Think of how many people flocked to hear Him speak. Ponder the huge crowds on the day of the triumphal entry into Jerusalem. He had a following, girl! People couldn't get enough of Jesus. They were magnetically drawn to Him, like children to the Pied Piper. Only, in this case, they weren't hypnotized. People were drawn by His magnetic grace. That's the thing about the love of God: it has the power to change people.

You can share that same grace with others. It's contagious, you know! Just love as Jesus loved and watch as people are won over by grace and truth.

I want to represent You, Jesus, so that others will follow my lead and turn to You. Amen.

A GRACE-FILLED CALLING

*Who saved us and called us to a holy calling, not because
of our works but because of his own purpose and grace,
which he gave us in Christ Jesus before the ages began.*
2 TIMOTHY 1:9 ESV

You have a holy calling on your life. Because of your faith in Jesus, He has placed His hand on you and His calling in your heart. You will follow hard after Him, not just now but forever. But what does it mean to "follow Jesus," exactly?

Imagine you got a phone call from a total stranger who said, "Hey, I have plans for you. Drop everything and come with me." Would you go? No way!

But Jesus won you over with His grace! He said, *"Girl, I see the pain you've struggled with. I see the empty feelings in your heart. I see the insecurities. And I adore you anyway."* Then He saved you and called you to give every part of your life to Him.

His actions are not the result of anything you've done. They are the result of everything He's done. He saved you. Gave you a new life. Set you free from the past. And, out of love and gratitude, you decided to take Him up on His offer to turn your life around. How could you resist so great a sacrifice?

*You've offered me grace, forgiveness, and a sense of
purpose. I'll gladly follow after You, Jesus! Amen.*

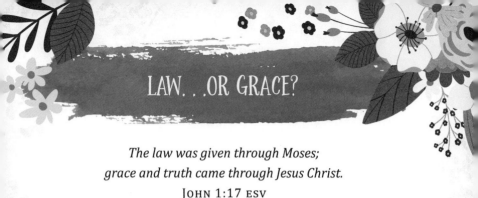

LAW. . .OR GRACE?

The law was given through Moses;
grace and truth came through Jesus Christ.
JOHN 1:17 ESV

Picture yourself at a fork in the road. To the right is a road that will make your life incredibly smooth. All you have to do is follow the clearly marked signs and stick to the path. To the left is a road filled with potholes, pain, and hard work. You're terrified just looking at it. How would you begin to navigate such a precarious road?

You wouldn't. You would take the road to the right, of course.

Only, not everyone does. Some people deliberately take the wrong road because they don't understand the bliss of grace. They think that the "law" path makes more sense because they want to earn their way into God's favor. If only they understood that all of the good works in the world won't get you there! The only way to find grace is to accept the sacrifice of Jesus Christ, the sinless Savior. When you do that, He provides a road straight to heaven. Best of all, He makes the journey with you, so you'll never have to be alone. That's a win-win!

Thank You for the grace road, Jesus.
I'm doing it Your way! Amen.

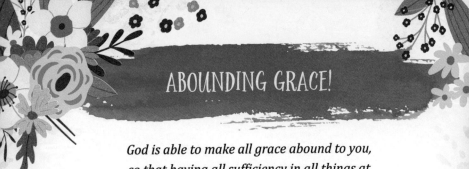

ABOUNDING GRACE!

God is able to make all grace abound to you,
so that having all sufficiency in all things at
all times, you may abound in every good work.
2 CORINTHIANS 9:8 ESV

Have you ever watched a group of kids at a trampoline park? It's over-whelming and a little terrifying, watching them leap and twirl in the air, one on top of the other. The opportunity for disaster is everywhere, especially with the heavy bouncers. You know the ones. They go down hard, they come up high. Over and over, they jump. They "abound."

In some ways, God's grace is like that high jump. It's a little dangerous. It has reached into the low lows of your sin and propelled you to a higher place, one you've never been before. It's showing you a new perspective, girl. It's abounding!

God loves and values you so much that He's willing to go deep in order for you to go high. So jump! Leap! Twirl! Allow the freedom of His Spirit to propel you to new heights as you place your trust in Him.

I get it, Lord! You found me worthy of grace, and You reached down to rescue me. How blessed I am! Amen.

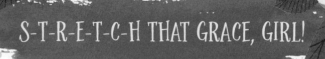

S-T-R-E-T-C-H THAT GRACE, GIRL!

Grow in the loving-favor that Christ gives you. Learn to know our Lord Jesus Christ better. He is the One Who saves. May He have all the shining-greatness now and forever. Let it be so.
2 PETER 3:18 NLV

If you've been up and down with your weight, you know the value of stretchy clothes. You can wear them at all sizes. Okay, so they only stretch so far, but at least you don't have to buy new things right away if you put on a few pounds.

God wants you to grow in His grace. That means you apply His goodness and His favor more and more over time. You don't just experience grace when you give your heart to Him. It's meant to grow your faith and make you a spiritual powerhouse.

He adores you. He values you above all other creation. (Puppies, cute as they are, don't stand a chance next to you!) So allow yourself to grow in Him. *S-t-r-e-t-c-h* your faith. Get to know Him better. His shining greatness is meant to turn you into a woman of great faith!

Lord, I get it! The grace I experienced at salvation was just the beginning. You've got so much more for me. I accept it, Jesus! Amen.

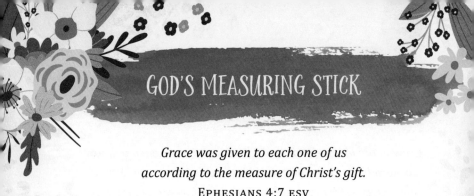

GOD'S MEASURING STICK

Grace was given to each one of us
according to the measure of Christ's gift.
Ephesians 4:7 esv

When you were a kid, your parents probably kept track of your height by using a measuring tape or measuring stick. Maybe there's a doorway in your house with markings on it from all of your different measurements. It's fun to watch kids grow!

Think about today's verse in light of those markings. God measures out how much grace He's going to give you. Now, you might read that and think, "Well, great. With my luck, He won't give me much!" Oh, but here's the truth: He doesn't base the measurement on anything you have or haven't done. (Whew!) Nope. He pours out grace according to the "measure of Christ's gift."

Whoa. The death of Jesus on the cross is the measuring stick! And, when you realize it goes to the heights, the depths, and the widths to cover your sin, you suddenly get it: His grace is immeasurable! It has no bounds. You will experience it every day in every way. What a remarkable God we serve.

Jesus, thank You for pouring out Your grace.
I love the way You measure! Amen.

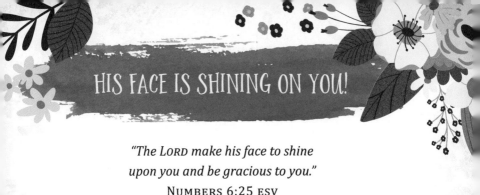

HIS FACE IS SHINING ON YOU!

"The LORD make his face to shine upon you and be gracious to you."
NUMBERS 6:25 ESV

Have you ever met someone who just seemed to glow? Of course, some girls have oily skin. They glow for other reasons. But the kind of glow we're talking about here is a heavenly glow. It's one that radiates from a peaceful smile or soft crinkles around the eyes when she laughs.

God's face is radiant. And according to this scripture from Numbers 6:25, His face is shining on you. You're catching brilliant beams of His glory and grace, girl.

What does that look like? Maybe you're having a rough day. Then, from out of the blue, a server at a fast-food restaurant looks your way, smiles, and says, "Have a blessed day!" In that moment, as you look at the light pouring from her eyes, you realize she's not the one speaking. God is. He's shining on you—through her.

And He can shine on others through you too! That's how His radiant grace works. Spread it far and wide. A smile. A hug. A laugh. A little goes a long, long way.

*Thanks for shining on me, Jesus!
I want to be a reflection of You. Amen.*

RICH IN EVERYTHING

You are rich in everything. You have faith. You can preach. You have much learning. You have a strong desire to help. And you have love for us. Now do what you should about giving also.

2 Corinthians 8:7 NLV

Today's verse says that you are rich in everything. Wait. . .*everything*, you ask? Like. . .*everything*?

God thinks you're worthy of the best, girl! So He lavishes His gifts on you. He's given you faith. He's given you the ability to share your story. He's placed a strong desire inside of you to help others. (And you thought that was just your idea!) He also placed love in your heart.

All of these things are holy gifts from a God who thinks you're awesome! He's made you rich—not so you can hoard it and keep it all to yourself, but so you can share with those you come in contact with. That faith? Your BFF needs some of it right now. That love? Your mom is going through a hard time and could use a dose of it. That desire to help? Your grandmother sure could use some help cleaning out her garage.

Spread grace around. God lavished it on you; now lavish it on others!

I want to be a grace spreader, Jesus! May I do my part to bring joy to everyone I meet. I want them to see You in me. Amen.

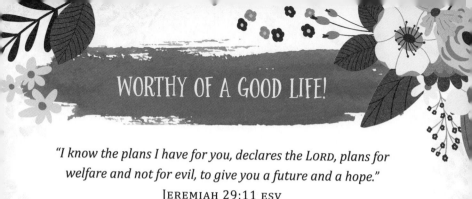

WORTHY OF A GOOD LIFE!

"I know the plans I have for you, declares the Lord, plans for welfare and not for evil, to give you a future and a hope."
JEREMIAH 29:11 ESV

God believes you're worthy of a good life. But what does that look like? Is He planning to lavish expensive cars and jewels on you? Does He have plans for you to live in a megamansion or hang out with movie stars?

Nope. Not that those things are necessarily bad, but God's idea of a good life definitely looks different from Hollywood's! His good life includes great plans for a wonderful future. A future where you're blessed. A future where you're spiritually and emotionally whole. A future where your family sticks together, rooted and grounded in Him.

God knows the plans. You don't. (That's the hard part: you have to trust Him.) But you do know this much: He has never let you down. He's never given you bad gifts. So you can trust that His vision of a "great future" is going to be pretty magnificent. That's how much He adores you, girl!

Lord, I trust You with my future. I know You've got awesome things planned for me. (Thanks!) I can't wait to see them come to pass. Amen.

HE WILL COMPLETE IT

So now finish doing it as well, so that your readiness in desiring it may he matched by your completing it out of what you have.
2 Corinthians 8:11 esv

Do you finish what you start? If you're like most girls, the answer might be, "Meh. Sometimes yes, sometimes no." It's so easy to start a project with zeal and gusto, but seeing it through to the end? Not so much.

Think of that big project you had to turn in last semester. You were excited. . .at first. Then your excitement fizzled out as the weeks went by, and you realized how much work it was going to be. You found yourself throwing it together the night before it was due. Ugh! (Don't you hate it when that happens?)

God's not a fan of procrastination either. But here's some amazing news: When it comes to His plans for you and for your future, He's going to finish what He started. You can count on it. And He'll do it on His perfect timetable. That's how much He adores you, girl! He thinks you're worthy of an amazing life.

I'm so excited about Your plans for my life, Jesus. I can't wait to see what You've got up Your sleeve! Amen.

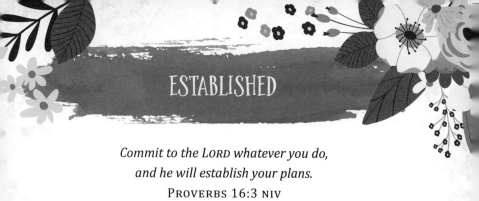

ESTABLISHED

Commit to the LORD whatever you do,
and he will establish your plans.
PROVERBS 16:3 NIV

Have you ever pondered the word *established*? Let's say you had a friend who was fighting for her life in the hospital. The family had no insurance, so you established an online fundraiser to bring in the necessary money for her care. You set it up. You spread the word. You kept it going. You saw it through until the bills were paid. In fact, you stayed on top of the details at every step.

That's how God approaches the plans for your life. When you commit to Him everything you do (and this requires daily prayer, because you do a l-o-t) then He will establish your plans. He'll set them up. Keep them going. See them through.

Everything starts with this word *commit*. To commit means you give it your all. You don't come into it halfhearted, wishy washy, unsure. Nope, you're 100 percent ready, and you fully plan to follow through.

Do you feel this strongly about the plans in front of you? If so, give them to the Lord and watch as He establishes them on your behalf!

I trust You to establish what I've committed to You, Jesus. Amen.

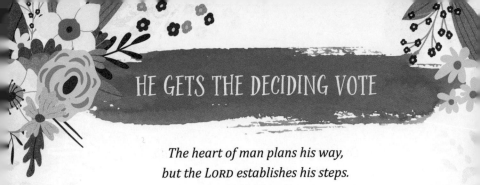

HE GETS THE DECIDING VOTE

The heart of man plans his way,
but the LORD establishes his steps.
PROVERBS 16:9 ESV

You've got all sorts of cool plans for your life. Maybe you've already decided what you want to be when you grow up. Where you'll go to college. What type of job you'll have. What sort of guy you plan to marry (if any). How many kids you'll have. You've got it all worked out.

Go ahead and make your plans, girl. But remember, God gets the deciding vote. This means you can't be shocked or upset if you don't get into the college of your dreams. It also means He might chart a completely different course for your career. And who knows! You might end up married to someone who's the polar opposite of what you imagined.

Keep your options open. Hold loosely to your plans. God might change them, but if He does, then you can rest assured that what He's got in mind is far superior to anything you might've cooked up on your own.

I get it, Lord! You love me so much that You always set the correct plans in action. I'll dream of how things could be, but I'll trust You if they don't work out exactly as I planned. Amen.

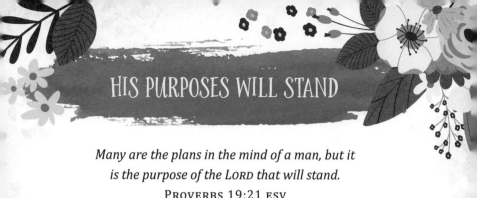

HIS PURPOSES WILL STAND

Many are the plans in the mind of a man, but it
is the purpose of the LORD that will stand.
PROVERBS 19:21 ESV

You'll make a lot of plans in this lifetime. What classes to take in school. Which friends to hang out with. Who to date. What school to attend. Which employer to say yes to. There will be opportunities on a daily basis to make plans, girl.

When you're on a roll, bouncing from thing to thing, it's easy to forget that God is ultimately the One in charge of those plans. Some days you'll just dive in, instinctively, without involving Him. Then, when things begin to go wrong, you'll have an "Oops!" moment where you realize you left Him out.

Just know this: God always has His way. Whether you choose to include Him or not, He always eventually leads you to where He planned for you to go in the first place. You can make it easy on yourself or hard on yourself. That's your choice. But it's always better to get His input before taking any steps forward. Just saying.

Sorry for leaving You out sometimes, Jesus. Your purposes are the ones that matter, not mine! Amen.

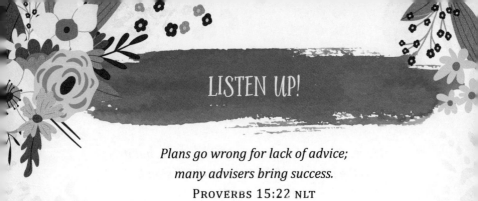

LISTEN UP!

Plans go wrong for lack of advice;
many advisers bring success.
PROVERBS 15:22 NLT

You've got a big decision to make. You're not sure which way to go. In many ways, it feels like you're standing at a fork in the road, and both ways look tempting. You pray, but you're still not 100 percent sure. Should you get advice? Who could help you?

Here's a fun fact about God: He doesn't just speak to *your* heart, He speaks to *all* believers. So if you ask a godly friend or adult for wise advice, she just might be able to give it if she's truly tuned in to God's voice.

Say you're trying to make a big decision about a job opportunity. You can't figure it out, because your school schedule is already nuts. You sit down with your school counselor, and she helps you put together a workable plan, one that leaves time for schoolwork, homework, the job, and even family activities. Whew! She thought of things you didn't!

Listen up when wise people offer advice. Pray about what they've shared (of course), but be open to suggestions.

Lord, You've got some wise people out there. I'll do my best to listen, especially when I don't know which way to go. Amen.

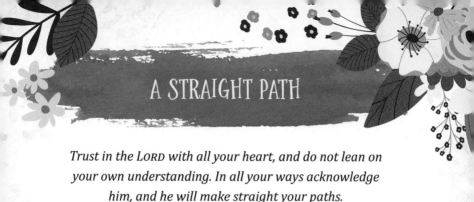

A STRAIGHT PATH

*Trust in the LORD with all your heart, and do not lean on
your own understanding. In all your ways acknowledge
him, and he will make straight your paths.*
PROVERBS 3:5–6 ESV

God can make your path straight. That's an amazing promise. If you've ever been on a crooked road, you know how vulnerable you feel! It twists and turns, goes up and down, and leaves you feeling discombobulated. But when you give God the reins, He straightens out the road in front of you and makes it clear which way to go. (And He provides safety as you travel.)

Why would He go to all of this trouble for you? After all, there are billions of people in the world. God is pretty busy, right?

Sure, He's busy, but He's never too busy for you! He adores you. And He's going to keep guiding you, no matter how busy He is with other things (like, say, world peace).

Giving *you* peace is just as important to Him. That's how much your heavenly Father values you!

*I get it, Lord. I matter to You. I matter so much that
You take the time to carve out a straight path and
watch over me as I travel along it. Thank You! Amen.*

HE'S MAKING IT CLEAR

The LORD answered me: "Write the vision; make it plain on tablets, so he may run who reads it."
HABAKKUK 2:2 ESV

God doesn't just have amazing plans for your life—He's also making them plain so you won't get confused! Check out what He said in today's verse from Habakkuk 2:2: "Write the vision; make it plain on tablets, so he may run who reads it."

Stop to think about a doctor writing a prescription. Sometimes the doctor's handwriting is so bad, you wonder how the pharmacist can read it! Maybe you even wonder if you'll end up with the right medication. When it comes to God, you never have to wonder. He makes His message clear!

So how and where do you read His messages? Start with the Bible. It's filled with clear-cut directions to show you how to live. Then pray! God speaks to His people in a still, small voice. He whispers instructions to your heart. He never wants you to be confused when He's giving the plans, so listen closely and do what He says.

Of course, God also speaks through people—your parents, friends, even your pastor or teacher. He's pretty good at giving them awesome advice for you.

I'll pay attention, Lord! When I do,
I know You will make it clear. Amen.

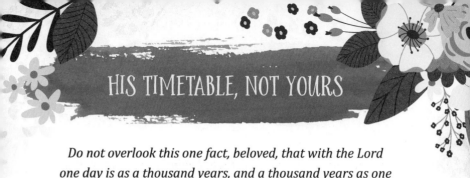

HIS TIMETABLE, NOT YOURS

Do not overlook this one fact, beloved, that with the Lord one day is as a thousand years, and a thousand years as one day. The Lord is not slow to fulfill his promise as some count slowness, but is patient toward you, not wishing that any should perish, but that all should reach repentance.

2 PETER 3:8–9 ESV

God has a completely different timetable than you, girl. It's true! You're human. When you want something, you want it now. And hey, the world has conditioned you to that idea. You can drive through and pick up fast food. With the internet, you have immediate access to information. You even put food in the microwave and it cooks up lickety-split.

When it comes to the things you're waiting on, however, results don't always come about so quickly. But before you give up and stop praying, remember: God knows the perfect timing to bring you the things you need. If He loves and values you as much as you know He does, don't you think you can trust Him with His timetable?

You can. You should.

Deep breath. God's buzzing along behind the scenes, working all things together for good.

I'll be patient, Lord! It's not easy, I confess, but I'll keep waiting on You. Amen.

HE'S WHISPERING DIRECTIONS (EVEN NOW!)

Your own ears will hear him. Right behind you a voice will say,
"This is the way you should go," whether to the right or to the left.
ISAIAH 30:21 NLT

God has amazing plans for your life, but you feel lost. Stuck. Confused. (Remember, confusion is from the enemy, not from your heavenly Father, so don't hang out there for very long!)

God wants to give you clear directions. *How,* you ask? He's whispering in your ear, even now. It's true! You might say, "Whoa. I don't hear a thing." But think about this: He spoke to men and women in the olden days, right? And the Bible says He's the same yesterday, today, and forever. So if He did it then, what makes you think He wouldn't speak now?

He's whispering through the voice of your parents. He's speaking through a close friend. He's giving directions through your circumstances. And His Spirit is actually speaking in that still, small voice of His to your heart. (This is how you "know" what to do, even when no one tells you—you discern it by His Spirit.)

God has given you everything you need to take steps in the right direction. Trust His plan. Follow His voice.

Lord, I trust You. I'm listening close.
I want to hear You loud and clear! Amen.

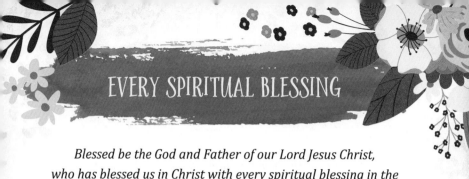

EVERY SPIRITUAL BLESSING

*Blessed be the God and Father of our Lord Jesus Christ,
who has blessed us in Christ with every spiritual blessing in the
heavenly places, even as he chose us in him before the foundation
of the world, that we should be holy and blameless before
him. In love he predestined us for adoption to himself as sons
through Jesus Christ, according to the purpose of his will.*
EPHESIANS 1:3–5 ESV

Life is a blessing. Your breath is a blessing! Health is a blessing. Those relationships you share—they're a blessing.

Every minute of every day is filled with blessings from God. And when you remember to view them that way, then your heart will be full. Grateful. Overflowing with confidence in the One who values you enough to make sure you're blessed. . .coming and going.

Today, if you're not feeling blessed, take the time to write down the many, many blessings you might be overlooking. For instance, you might write down: *Food in the pantry. Healthy family. My dad's job. Great Christian friends.*

There are many, many blessings, if only you will see them for what they are. God has mapped out a great plan for your life, and He desires to bless you at every turn.

*Thank You for loving me so much that You pour out blessings,
Lord! I'm so grateful for Your tender, loving care. Amen.*

TRANSFORMED TO LIVE AN AMAZING LIFE

Don't copy the behavior and customs of this world,
but let God transform you into a new person by changing
the way you think. Then you will learn to know God's will
for you, which is good and pleasing and perfect.
ROMANS 12:2 NLT

Have you ever wondered why God wants to see your heart and mind transformed? Why is He so keen on you not looking like—or acting like—the people in this world? Is He out to ruin your fun? Does He want to force you to live a strict, rules-first life?

Nope. None of that! He knows a secret that you likely haven't figured out yet: life is easier when you think and act like Him. When your mind is transformed and becomes more like His and less like the world's, you'll live a safer, more controlled life. God's will is not about rules; it's about relationship with the One who knows you best and loves you most!

If God cared enough about you to transform your thinking, then no doubt He has amazing plans for your future. Trust Him, girl. But start by giving Him your thoughts, your heart, and your attitude!

Lord, I give myself to You. Transform me!
Make me into Your image so that things
will go well in my life. I trust You! Amen.

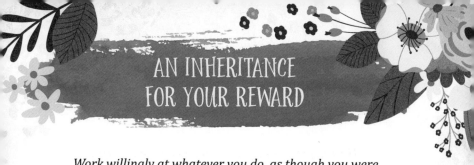

AN INHERITANCE
FOR YOUR REWARD

Work willingly at whatever you do, as though you were
working for the Lord rather than for people. Remember
that the Lord will give you an inheritance as your reward,
and that the Master you are serving is Christ.
Colossians 3:23–24 nlt

Have you ever received an inheritance? Maybe one of your grandparents passed away and you received a token, something that once belonged to them. A quilt. A piece of jewelry. Money.

People leave behind all sorts of things as an inheritance, but Jesus left the very best thing of all—worth far more than a diamond ring or a car. He left the promise of eternity, a "forever" experience with Him. (Hey, no one else left you that, did they?)

So work hard in this wonderful life God has given you, but remember: there's an even better life coming. Christians don't have to fear death. We have heaven to look forward to! Heaven is our reward for falling in love with Jesus and giving our hearts to Him.

Work for Him, not people. He's leaving you a crown that will sparkle longer than any earthly jewelry you might receive.

Thank You for the reward of heaven, Jesus!
Nothing even comes close. Amen.

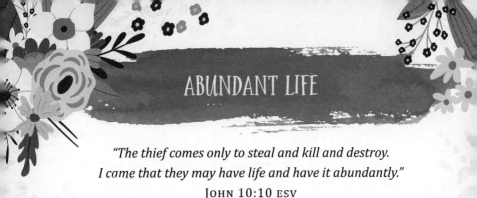

ABUNDANT LIFE

"The thief comes only to steal and kill and destroy.
I came that they may have life and have it abundantly."
JOHN 10:10 ESV

The enemy of your soul wants you to believe that God doesn't care about your future. He's sneaky, that one! He whispers things in your ear like, "Hey, you think God cares about you? Wrong! If He did, then your loved one wouldn't have died" or "God's not interested in you. He's got bigger issues to deal with."

Those are lies from the pit of hell, girl! God does care. He does have good plans for you. And He's working them out, even now. The life in front of you isn't going to be *blah* either. It's going to be abundant! That's a promise from today's scripture. So if things aren't feeling abundant right now, put the circumstances in perspective. Recognize who's trying to zap your joy (the enemy) and who's standing right there, ready to pour out hope (Jesus).

Jesus came to bring life. Abundant, joy-filled, precious life.

Thank You, Jesus, for offering me abundant life! You're not the one stealing from me. I can trust You with the plans for my future because You love me so much! Amen.

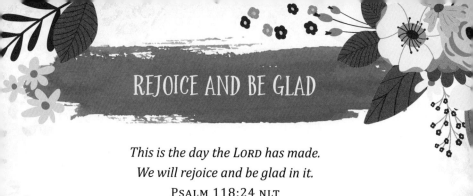

REJOICE AND BE GLAD

This is the day the LORD has made.
We will rejoice and be glad in it.
PSALM 118:24 NLT

Not every day has you jumping up and down with glee. Some days you just want to hide under the covers and forget about everything. Ugh! Today's verse is a good reminder that God wants you to keep those icky days in perspective. After all, there's more good than bad. There's more happy than sad. There's more hope than despair. There's more peace than turmoil.

Really, when you think about it that way, you have to confess that bad days, especially the *really* bad ones, are pretty rare. Most days, things don't go wrong. People don't pass away. You don't panic. Most days are just. . .normal.

But here's the thing: whether you're having a good day or bad, God hasn't fallen off of His throne. He's right there, and He's got complete control of your day. Those things that feel out of your control? They totally are, but they're not out of God's.

He's got great plans for you. That's how much He adores you. And you can trust Him to carry out those plans, even on the bad days.

I give my days to You, Jesus, good and bad!
Thanks for loving me so much. Amen.

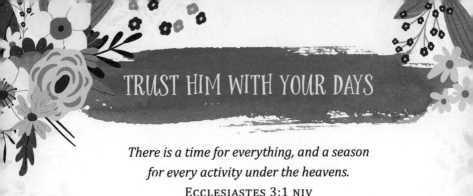

TRUST HIM WITH YOUR DAYS

*There is a time for everything, and a season
for every activity under the heavens.*
ECCLESIASTES 3:1 NIV

This familiar verse from Ecclesiastes tells us that there's a time for everything. The scripture goes on to say there's a time to be born, a time to die, a time to plant, a time to harvest. God has (literally) ordained times for everything you could think of. He's on the job, girl!

Why, then, would you doubt Him when it comes to your days? He's got it all mapped out. There's a time for all of the things you're going to accomplish. There's a season for every relationship. Your activities are in His hands.

You can trust God with your days, girl. His heavenly clock has it all worked out, even if you can't see what's going on behind the scenes.

What season are you in? Trust Him in it, good or bad. He's got this. He's got you.

You're always on the clock, Lord! You have a time and a season for everything I will ever go through. I know I can trust You with my days, and today I choose to do just that. Amen.

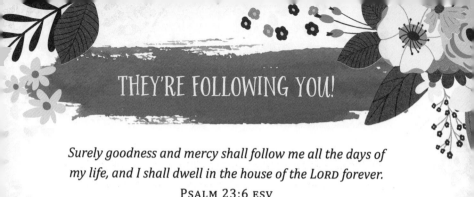

THEY'RE FOLLOWING YOU!

*Surely goodness and mercy shall follow me all the days of
my life, and I shall dwell in the house of the LORD forever.*
PSALM 23:6 ESV

What's following you, you ask? Goodness and mercy! They're chasing
you down, like a runner coming down the track. The goodness of God
is yours for the taking, girl. All of His blessings, all of His love, all of His
best. . .all for you! And His mercy—oh, how He pours it out, even when
you don't deserve it.

Say you've done something awful. Truly awful. No one knows but
you. Then your dirty little secret is discovered. There's no hiding it. Before long, your parents find out. You're disciplined, but their response
isn't as harsh as you feared. In fact, they tell you—in spite of their
disappointment—that they love and forgive you.

Whoa. You never saw that one coming. And the mercy they've ex-
tended makes you want to do better next time.

That's what God's goodness and mercy do too. You want to do better next time. And even better the time after that. Goodness and mercy
propel you down the track toward a first-place finish.

*Lord, thank You for chasing me down with Your
goodness and mercy. I'm so grateful. Amen.*

GOD'S GIFT TO YOU, HIS DAUGHTER

*I concluded there is nothing better than to be happy and enjoy
ourselves as long as we can. And people should eat and drink
and enjoy the fruits of their labor, for these are gifts from God.*
ECCLESIASTES 3:12–13 NLT

You are worthy, girl! Worthy of what, you ask? A good life! A great future. And lots and lots of great days, poured out from your heavenly Father above.

Take a look at today's verse. God knows you work hard. He sees how hard your parents work too. But if you think He's all about the work, think again! His gifts to His kids include the rewards of their work.

Wondering what that means? When your dad brings home his paycheck, that money is used to buy food. And to pay the mortgage. And to get your school clothes. . .and so on. Those things are the rewards of his diligent work.

God has rewards for your work too! It might look like an A on your report card instead of a B. Or it might look like a new cell phone after you worked hard to help around the house. One way or the other, you'll be blessed, girl!

*Thank You for those fun and unexpected rewards,
Jesus! They make my heart happy. Amen.*

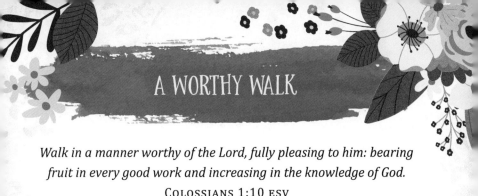

A WORTHY WALK

*Walk in a manner worthy of the Lord, fully pleasing to him: bearing
fruit in every good work and increasing in the knowledge of God.*
Colossians 1:10 esv

God sees you as worthy—of love, care, gifts, joy, and so on. He adores
you! You might read this and think, *Wow, it's all on Him! I can live the way
I want, and He'll go right on finding me worthy now that I'm a believer.*

Well, that's true, but. . .don't you want to make His heart happy? Aren't
you interested in drawing others to Him?

Today's verse sheds some light on how God feels His worthy ones
should live. He wants you to "walk in a manner worthy of the Lord." But
what does that mean exactly?

It means you bear some responsibility to do the right thing, girl!
Your life needs to line up with the Bible. You need to have the attributes
of Christ. Does this mean you're expected to be perfect? Not even close!
Does it mean you should be making an effort to be more godly? Absolutely.

Walk in a manner worthy of your calling. You can do it. You *really* can.

I'll do my best, Lord! I want to be more like You. Amen.

WORTHY OF THE GOSPEL

Only let your manner of life be worthy of the gospel of Christ,
so that whether I come and see you or am absent, I may
hear of you that you are standing firm in one spirit, with one
mind striving side by side for the faith of the gospel.
PHILIPPIANS 1:27 ESV

Today's verse says that your life must be worthy of the Gospel of Christ. That means your life has to line up with the salvation message.

Jesus gave His all for you. Literally, His *all*. He died on the cross and took your sin. The least you can do as a believer is to live in a way that reflects the salvation message.

So what does that look like? It means not being a hypocrite. Don't say one thing on Sunday and live a different way on Monday. It means actually reading your Bible and putting your faith in Him, not just acting like it. Basically, it means living in a way that says, "Jesus, I totally believe Your sacrifice was worth it." After all, you didn't just give your heart to Him so that you could go to heaven one day. You gave Him your heart because you wanted a relationship—here and now.

Jesus, I want to live in a way that
shares the Gospel message! Amen.

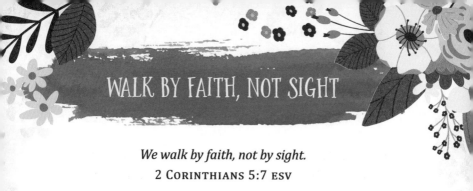

WALK BY FAITH, NOT SIGHT

We walk by faith, not by sight.
2 CORINTHIANS 5:7 ESV

The road is tricky, and the enemy of your soul is trying to get you off course. So how does a worthy girl walk? She walks by faith, not by sight.

How do you do that?

Say you're in a crisis. Your father has lost his job. He's behind on the mortgage. The mortgage company is threatening to foreclose. Do you panic? Do you immediately assume your family will be living on the street? No. You pray. And you believe with your whole heart that the God of the universe—the same One who created and adores you—has a plan. He's got a solution. And that solution will be for your good, not evil.

It's easier to walk by sight than to live by faith. That's what most people do! They see their circumstances and panic. But not you, girl! You might have a moment of fear, but you get over it quickly and begin to walk in a way that points others to Christ.

Lord, I choose to walk by faith, even when the circumstances swirling around me are bad. I trust You, Jesus! Amen.

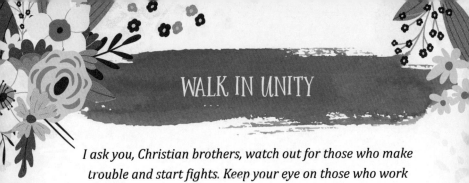

WALK IN UNITY

I ask you, Christian brothers, watch out for those who make trouble and start fights. Keep your eye on those who work against the teaching you received. Keep away from them.

ROMANS 16:17 NLV

A worthy girl walks in unity with those who take a stand for the Bible and for God. She doesn't hide in the corner when people ask, "Hey, are you one of those Christians?" She's bold in her faith and lives in a way that points to Jesus.

She is careful not to end up in quarrels or fights with other believers. (Hey, she's on to the devil's schemes! He wants to divide the body of Christ, but she's not having it!)

One thing is for sure—she's sticking to what she's learned. She's not letting the world's philosophies pull her away from what the Bible says is true. Oh, it's tempting, but she's not giving in just to be popular or to avoid trouble. She'd rather stick up for truth than break God's heart with a lie.

You can do it, girl. Walk in unity with the Word. Walk in unity with Jesus. Walk in unity with like-minded believers.

I'm sticking up for You and Your Word, Jesus! Amen.

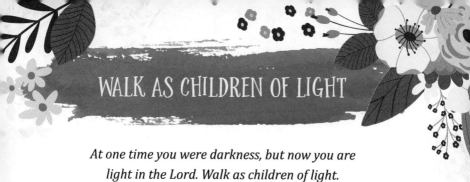

WALK AS CHILDREN OF LIGHT

At one time you were darkness, but now you are
light in the Lord. Walk as children of light.
EPHESIANS 5:8 ESV

A worthy girl walks as a child of the Light. Think about it like this: Before you became a Christian, how did you live? For yourself, right? To please your friends too, no doubt. You pretty much just did what you wanted when you wanted it. But that sort of lifestyle is driven by darkness. It's not focused on Jesus.

Then you gave your heart to Him. (You have done that, right?) From that moment on, everything changed! A Christian girl lives as a child of the Light. She makes decisions based on her relationship with Jesus. She asks herself questions like, "What would Jesus do?" or "What would please His heart?" She's always thinking of Him, not herself.

You were once in darkness, but now you're in the light. In fact, you *are* the light! You're shining brightly for all the world to see, girl. So shine on!

I want to shine for You, Jesus, not draw attention to myself. I used to have a me, myself, and I lifestyle, but those days are behind me now. It's all about You! Amen.

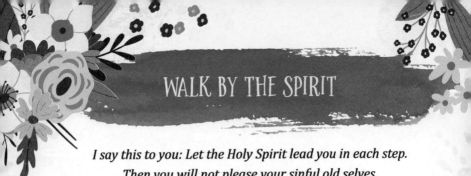

WALK BY THE SPIRIT

I say this to you: Let the Holy Spirit lead you in each step.
Then you will not please your sinful old selves.
GALATIANS 5:16 NLV

As you set off on your walk through this life, you need a guide. (It would never work to set off on a journey if you didn't have some idea where you were going, right?)

So what sort of map or guide do you use to get from place to place? Of course, God wants you to use the Bible. It's loaded with great road markers to guide you toward a more successful Christian life. But there's another compass you can use as well.

The Holy Spirit was given to you as a gift. He's your comforter, your discerner, and your guide. He came to live in your heart when you became a Christian, and He's that internal compass guiding you to the right or the left. When you have a big decision to make, He's the One whispering, *"Go to the right!"*

God adores you. In fact, He values you so much that He gave you His Spirit so that you would never, ever have to be lost.

Thanks for guiding me, Holy Spirit!
I wouldn't make it without You! Amen.

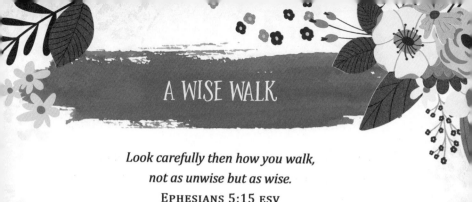

A WISE WALK

Look carefully then how you walk,
not as unwise but as wise.
EPHESIANS 5:15 ESV

How would you define the word *foolish*? Does a foolish person pay much attention to the outcome, or does she just dive in without any thought for how things will turn out in the end?

Lots of girls are foolish these days. They want what they want, and they jump right in to get it—never worrying about who they will hurt or what devastating consequences their actions might have. As long as they get their way, they're happy.

You're not like that. Because you're a Jesus girl, you walk wisely. You're careful. You're thinking ahead. You're paying attention to who might be hurt by your decisions. And most of all, you're thinking about how your choices will affect your relationship with God. You don't want anything to get in the way of that.

God wants you to be wise in how you walk. Eyes wide open. Ears listening. Heart tuned in to hear His voice. Not thinking of yourself, but always thinking of Him.

I want to be wise in this life, Jesus. May I never foolishly plow ahead, thinking only of myself! Amen.

A PATIENT WALK

They who wait upon the Lord will get new strength. They will rise up with wings like eagles. They will run and not get tired. They will walk and not become weak.
ISAIAH 40:31 NLV

Patience, girl! Patience! Maybe you've heard those words. No doubt your parents have spoken them when you got in a hurry. Or maybe your teacher suggested you use more patience when dealing with a fellow student. (Hey, life gives you all sorts of opportunities to exhibit more patience, right?)

Think of a time when you forgot to use your patience. Who got hurt? No doubt lots of people, yourself included. Impatient people hurt people. They push. They shove. They demand. They are only interested in getting what they want on their timeline.

God's timeline is *always* different from our own. Maybe that's why today's verse is so clear: wait on Him. When you do, He will renew your strength. In fact, you'll be so strong that you can mount up like an eagle and take off flying! Wow! That's a wonderful benefit of exhibiting patience, isn't it?

I'll be more patient, Lord. Okay, okay. . .I'll need Your help to do this, but I trust in You. Amen.

A WEIGHTLESS WALK

Therefore, since we are surrounded by such a huge crowd of witnesses to the life of faith, let us strip off every weight that slows us down, especially the sin that so easily trips us up. And let us run with endurance the race God has set before us. We do this by keeping our eyes on Jesus, the champion who initiates and perfects our faith. Because of the joy awaiting him, he endured the cross, disregarding its shame. Now he is seated in the place of honor beside God's throne.
HEBREWS 12:1–2 NLT

Imagine you're a runner in a race. Before starting, you strap on a backpack filled with several bags of flour. You're completely weighted down, but you do your best to run as fast as you can. You end up falling behind the rest of the pack, and you also begin to experience pain as the weight wears you down.

Here's a question to ponder: Why? Why would you do that to yourself? Knowing the weights will cause you to stumble and possibly fall, why would you load them into that backpack in the first place?

That's what you do when you decide to carry the weight of the world on your shoulders. Jesus wants you to give those things to Him, girl! You were never meant to carry them. So let them go.

I'll do my best to let go, Jesus. Amen.

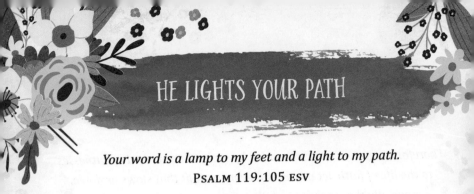

HE LIGHTS YOUR PATH

Your word is a lamp to my feet and a light to my path.
PSALM 119:105 ESV

Imagine you were asked to run a marathon in the middle of the night. Without lights. You had to take off from point A and make it to point B without any instructions or any streetlights overhead. The task would be impossible! No doubt you would trip and fall a dozen times, at least.

A lot of people try to navigate their way through life like that. They could ask for help from Jesus to light their path, but they decide to go their own way. Then they wonder why they fall into potholes along the way!

The Word of God (the Bible) is a lamp to your feet and a light to your path. When you're feeling completely blinded by the world, you can turn to the Bible and find the light you need to keep moving forward. All of the answers you're seeking are found in that amazing book. So don't run in the dark, girl! Toss those night goggles and reach for the real illumination, the Word of God!

I'll look to You and Your Word, Lord!
I'll stop trying to do things on my own. Amen.

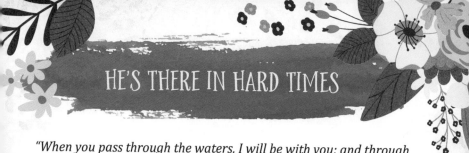

HE'S THERE IN HARD TIMES

"When you pass through the waters, I will be with you; and through the rivers, they shall not overwhelm you; when you walk through fire you shall not be burned, and the flame shall not consume you."

ISAIAH 43:2 ESV

You've been through a lot. You've seen something you wish you hadn't. Been through some challenges you'd rather forget. And yet, you're still here. You're still going. And God wants you to know that He was right there with you, even in the hardest of times.

Did you realize that God actually carries you during the hardest of times? He lifts you out of flood waters. He carries you through the fire. And, if you take a close look at today's verse, you'll see that you can come through those things unscathed (basically, without the smell of smoke in your hair).

How is such a thing possible? When God takes control, He can pull you through a dark situation and heal you from the inside out. He can take the nastiness you experienced and wash it away, removing the pain and lingering effects.

He was with you every step of the way, girl. That's how much He loves you. And He doesn't plan to leave you hanging now!

Thanks for carrying me through the flood and the fire, Jesus. Whew! I've been through some stuff. If not for You, there's no telling where I'd be. Amen.

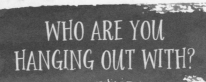

WHO ARE YOU HANGING OUT WITH?

Whoever walks with the wise becomes wise, but the companion of fools will suffer harm. Disaster pursues sinners, but the righteous are rewarded with good.
PROVERBS 13:20–21 ESV

Let's talk about the people you hang out with. Sure, a few of them are fine. Maybe *most*, even. There's the one girl (you know the one) who's a piece of work, but she's mostly harmless.

Then there are the others. They're harder to get along with. They are always trying to talk you into doing things you shouldn't. It's like they can't wait to see you fall. But you're on to them. You know their tricks. They've got a plan to drag you down with them.

Walk with the wise. That's the point of today's scripture. And hey, you know it's true that you become more like who you hang out with. When you spend time with quality people, you raise your own standards. Hang out with the not-so-great ones, and, well. . .

So here's a question: When people hang out with you, do they come away from the experience with raised standards? You want to set an example for all. They're counting on you to lead in a godly way. (They know you're a Christian, right?)

Lord, I'll hang out with good people. I want to grow and remain strong. And I'll be a good example to others as best I can! Amen.

OUT OF DARKNESS

*You are a chosen people, a royal priesthood, a holy nation,
God's special possession, that you may declare the praises of
him who called you out of darkness into his wonderful light.*
1 PETER 2:9 NIV

Have you ever been in a really dark room? Maybe you woke up in the middle of the night because you heard a younger sibling crying from down the hallway. You stumbled out of bed, flipped on the light, and the sudden shock of the overhead glow nearly blinded you.

That's kind of how it is for people who've been walking in spiritual darkness when they come to Jesus. It can be kind of shocking. Jarring! They aren't used to it. That's why you have to be patient—with yourself and with others. They won't always get it right the first time. Their eyes are just getting adjusted to walking with Jesus.

God has brought you out of the darkness, girl. You have seen some icky stuff. Some of your friends and loved ones are still involved in icky stuff. But Jesus has set you on a bright path. Don't get overwhelmed by the light. Just rest in the confidence that He loves you so much that He chose you to be His.

*Thanks for putting me on a bright path, Jesus! My eyes
are getting used to the light now. I like it here! Amen.*

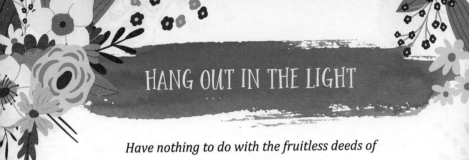

HANG OUT IN THE LIGHT

*Have nothing to do with the fruitless deeds of
darkness, but rather expose them.*
EPHESIANS 5:11 NIV

Today's scripture is an interesting one. You know you're not really supposed to be hanging out with not-so-great people, the ones trying to drag you down a wrong path. But, as one of God's worthy girls, you also have an obligation to expose fruitless deeds of darkness.

Ugh. Does that mean you have to shine a spotlight on the bad things your friends are doing? Are you supposed to tell on them, to stop them from moving forward with their evil plans?

Sometimes that's exactly what needs to happen. But here's another way of looking at this verse. You can pray for them. Pray that God will bring their sin into the light. (He can do a far better job of that than you ever could, anyway.) When He exposes something, it's undeniable. Contrast that with you "telling on" a friend. Sometimes the teller is believed; sometimes she's not.

God's pretty good at exposing things. So pray, girl. Stay away from the wrong crowd. And watch as the Lord brings correction to them.

*Lord, I'll stay away from that crowd. And I'll do my best
to shine a light on what's going on, even if it means
I leave it in Your (very capable) hands. Amen.*

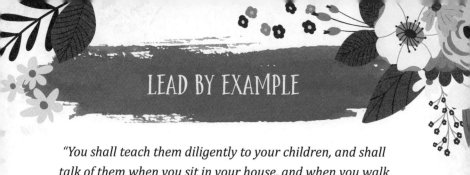

LEAD BY EXAMPLE

"You shall teach them diligently to your children, and shall talk of them when you sit in your house, and when you walk by the way, and when you lie down, and when you rise."

DEUTERONOMY 6:7 ESV

God calls you worthy. And you're thrilled to be one of His kids! But wouldn't it be great if you could bring your friends and loved ones along for the ride? Don't you want them to enjoy freedom in Christ too?

They can! And you can lead by example. Take a look at today's verse. It's a challenge to parents, asking them to teach God's laws to their children. But you can also use this verse as a challenge to set an example to your friends and younger siblings.

How do you do that? First, don't be a hypocrite. Oh, it's not easy. That's for sure. You sometimes snap at your younger sister or argue with your friend. But if you're saying, "I'm a Christian" out of one side of your mouth and snapping at them out of the other, you're sending a confusing message, girl! Let God's laws (the things you've learned from the Bible and from walking with Him) resonate in everything you say and do. Then you really *are* leading by example!

I'll talk about the things I've learned, Jesus! And I'll do my best to live them out. I don't want to be a hypocrite, but I'll definitely need Your help with this one. Amen.

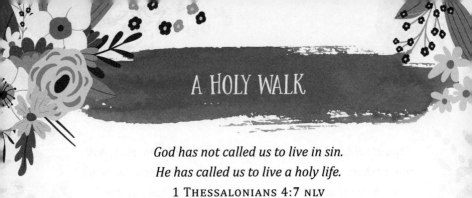

A HOLY WALK

God has not called us to live in sin.
He has called us to live a holy life.
1 THESSALONIANS 4:7 NLV

Holiness. It's an amazing word, isn't it? Maybe you look at that word and think, *Yeah, that's beyond me. I could never live a holy life!* Maybe you've tried and (according to your own estimation) failed.

Here's the truth: we all fail at holiness. We're human. We mess up. "All have sinned and fall short of the glory of God" (Romans 3:23 ESV). That's why we need Jesus so much! And here's some good news—He never fails the holiness test. Never. Ever. So when you give your heart to Him, when His Spirit comes to live inside of you, His holiness takes over.

It's not on you, girl, but you do have to walk it out. You have to try to live a holy life. You have to walk according to the purposes He's established. Stay away from sin. Don't engage in wicked behavior. And hang tight to Jesus in good times and bad.

The road ahead of you is a holy walkway, but you can travel it if you trust Him to live through you.

I get it, Jesus. I'll stay away from sin and stick close to You. You give me the power to live in holiness. I love it! Amen.

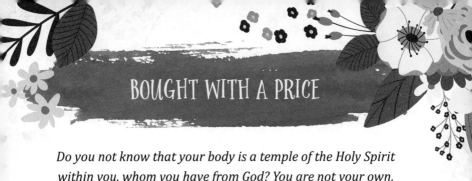

BOUGHT WITH A PRICE

Do you not know that your body is a temple of the Holy Spirit within you, whom you have from God? You are not your own, for you were bought with a price. So glorify God in your body.
1 Corinthians 6:19–20 esv

If you've ever been to an auction, you know the excitement that can build as bidding wars get underway. People fight one another, making higher bids, to take the prize.

Now picture yourself on the auction block. You're up for sale. And the devil is fighting it out with God. The devil wants you. God wants you. And, in the end, God places the highest bid anyone has ever seen—He offers His Son as a sacrifice for your sin. He buys you, once and for all.

Wow! When you think of it like that, does it make you want to honor Him more with the way you live? You were bought with a price, girl! And you are a temple of the Holy Spirit, which means that He's living inside of you, even now.

So how you live matters. How you love matters. What you say and do matters. *Every single moment* matters because you were purchased at such a high price.

I get it, Jesus. I was on the auction block, and You bought me with Your very life. I'll do my best to honor You with mine. Amen.

DON'T MAKE ME BEG!

*We pleaded with you, encouraged you, and urged you to
live your lives in a way that God would consider worthy.
For he called you to share in his Kingdom and glory.*
1 THESSALONIANS 2:12 NLT

The apostles risked their lives to spread the Gospel message. They traveled from city to city, area to area, sharing the message of what Jesus did for them. Many ended up in prison. Others were martyred for their faith. They (literally) gave their all.

How sad, then, that they had to often resort to begging their new converts to live right. (Quite a contrast, right? Some risked all; others weren't willing to risk much.)

It's the same today. Some people are fully in. They give their hearts to the Lord and dive headfirst into a relationship with Him, taking it seriously. Other people? Not so much. You can encourage them, plead with them, and even insist that they live a godly life, but you can't make them. No one can.

You, though? You don't need anyone to beg. You don't need anyone to twist your arm. You're in this to win this. You've fallen head over heels in love with Jesus and want to honor Him with all you do. Now that's a great way to live!

*I won't make You beg, Jesus. I'll do my best, simply because
I love You and want to live in a way that pleases You. Amen.*

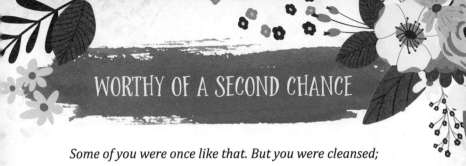

WORTHY OF A SECOND CHANCE

Some of you were once like that. But you were cleansed;
you were made holy; you were made right with God by calling
on the name of the Lord Jesus Christ and by the Spirit of our God.
1 Corinthians 6:11 nlt

God thinks you're worthy of a do-over. That's right, girl! He's going to give you second chances. And third. And fourth. That's how merciful and gracious He is.

Does this mean you should deliberately disobey or mess up, since you know He's going to forgive you anyway? Of course not! Flat-out disobedience would be wrong. But if you do slip up and do something wrong, God is right there, ready to forgive and give you another opportunity to get it right.

Why do you suppose God is in the "second chances" business? Why not just punish you when you mess up? Wouldn't you learn from your mistakes? Maybe, but at what cost? He would be pushing you away if He always came down hard on you. You would stop trusting Him if He never showed mercy and grace. He wants you to know that you are valuable to Him. You are His child, after all!

Thanks for offering second chances, Lord! Amen.

FIX YOUR THOUGHTS

Now, dear brothers and sisters, one final thing. Fix your thoughts on what is true, and honorable, and right, and pure, and lovely, and admirable. Think about things that are excellent and worthy of praise.
PHILIPPIANS 4:8 NLT

Have you ever used superglue? Maybe you tried and ended up getting your fingers stuck together. (It happens!)

Today's verse shares a fun concept: God wants you to superglue your thoughts to His Word. "Fix" your thoughts on what is true and honorable and right and pure and lovely and admirable. In other words, remain focused (fixated) on the good things, not the bad. When you spend your time thinking about things that are excellent (as opposed to, say, all of the evil going on around you), you won't get so bogged down in the icky stuff.

It's not always easy. There's very real stuff happening. (Don't believe it? Turn on the news for five minutes, and you'll see!) People are angry. They argue. They fight over politics and all sorts of things.

But you? You're not engaging in those fights. Your thoughts are superglued to Jesus. You have His heart, His message, and His mindset. You're able to see beyond the mess to the bliss of loving Him.

I'm supergluing my thoughts to Your Word, Jesus! Amen.

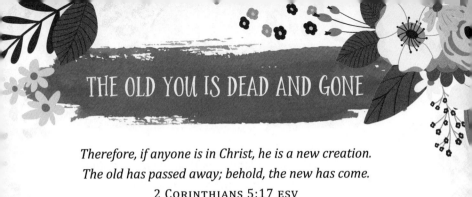

THE OLD YOU IS DEAD AND GONE

Therefore, if anyone is in Christ, he is a new creation.
The old has passed away; behold, the new has come.
2 CORINTHIANS 5:17 ESV

Did you realize you died and rose again, just like Jesus? It's true.

How, you ask? If you're a believer in Jesus, if you've truly given your heart to Him, then He took the old you (the one with the shame, the guilt, and the pain) and buried her under the covering of His blood. He tossed your sins as far as the east is from the west. When He came to live inside of you, you were reborn, girl. No, really. The old you is gone. The new you is here for good!

It's an interesting concept, but it's true. There's no more "old" you. There's only the new and improved version, the one He wants to present to the world. Now you see why it's so important to live a holy life! You can't go on living like you used to. That girl is gone. The girl who lives now is a reflection of the Creator of the world! She's got to shine bright for all the world to see.

All things are made new in Christ, even you!

I get it, Jesus! You made me brand-new! I won't live like the old me. I'm now the new me. Amen.

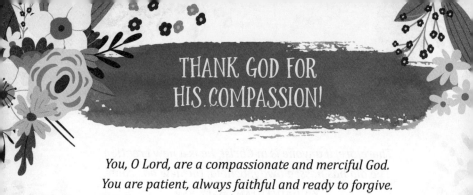

THANK GOD FOR HIS COMPASSION!

You, O Lord, are a compassionate and merciful God.
You are patient, always faithful and ready to forgive.
PSALM 86:15 GW

How many times has God given you second chances? Too many to count, right? Have you ever wondered why He's so compassionate and merciful? Why He's always patient and ready to forgive? It's in His nature, girl! And because you're created in His image, it's in your nature too. He wants you to treat others that way.

Think of it this way: If you had a toddler who kept bumping into things and breaking them, would you continue to scold? No doubt you would remove the items and then train the child—with love and compassion leading the way. Your ultimate goal wouldn't be the things but the child. That's how love works!

God is that loving parent. He's compassionate. He wants the best for you. And even when you bump into things and make a mess, He's not mad. He just moves them over, hugs you, and says, *"Try again, girl!"*

Thank You, Jesus, for Your compassion and mercy!
I don't know why You keep forgiving me for the
mess-ups, but I'm so glad You do. Amen.

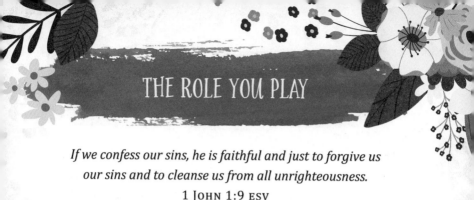

THE ROLE YOU PLAY

If we confess our sins, he is faithful and just to forgive us our sins and to cleanse us from all unrighteousness.
1 JOHN 1:9 ESV

God is the One who gives second chances, but you have a role to play too.

What role, you ask? Start with asking for forgiveness when you mess up. Hey, there's a conditional word in today's verse: *if*. If you confess your sins, He will be faithful to forgive.

So what happens if you don't?

When Jesus died on the cross, He died for all sin, but God wants your heart, girl. He wants you to actually recognize and acknowledge when you mess up. So get it off your chest. Come to Him. This process is good for you. It reminds you that He's approachable. It's also a great reminder that He wants you on days when you're behaving and days when you're not.

You can't forgive your own sin. You can't give yourself a second chance. But you can activate the process by confessing and then receiving God's mercy and grace.

Thank You for giving me opportunities to get it right, Jesus. I come to You today with some things I need to talk about. Here goes. . . Amen.

NEW EVERY MORNING

This I remember, and so I have hope. It is because of the Lord's loving-kindness that we are not destroyed for His loving-pity never ends. It is new every morning. He is so very faithful.
LAMENTATIONS 3:21–23 NLV

Have you ever noticed that a brand-new day puts new hope in your heart? Say you spent all day Tuesday fretting over a situation with a friend. But then, randomly, you woke up on Wednesday morning and it was the farthest thing from your mind. Somehow, in the night, you let it go.

God wants to remind you today that His mercies are new every single morning. Every day is a fresh start, a chance to begin again. (That's 365 second chances a year, for those who are keeping track!)

It should give you hope to know that the Creator of the universe knows how to re-create your heart every single day. And He does so out of loving-kindness toward you. Each new morning, He glances down at you with love in His eyes and says, *"I'm crazy about this one!"* Then, with great joy, He offers a fresh, new start.

I'm so grateful for new chances and new days, Lord. Bye-bye yesterday. Glad you're gone! Amen.

FORGET ABOUT IT!

Forget what happened in the past, and do
not dwell on events from long ago.
ISAIAH 43:18 GW

"Just forget about it!"

Maybe you've heard those words. Maybe you've spoken them. Imagine you've borrowed a pen from the girl who sits next to you in your Spanish class. She asks about it the following day, but you realize you must have lost it somewhere. When you tell her, she says, "Oh, don't worry about it! Just forget about it!"

It's not a big deal to her. In fact, she really doesn't care at all.

That's how you should view your past, girl. It's behind you now. It's in the rearview mirror. Sure, you messed up. You were a different person back then. But now? Now you're focused on today and aiming toward tomorrow. You don't have time to get bogged down in all of the junk from yesterday.

Forget about it.

Sure, it matters. And yes, there might be some consequences. But don't let guilt and condemnation rob you of the joy of today. Jesus wants His girls to walk with a forward posture, not a backward one!

I won't keep looking back over my shoulder, Jesus.
I'm so grateful for Your forgiveness. Thanks for
helping me let go of my yesterdays. Amen.

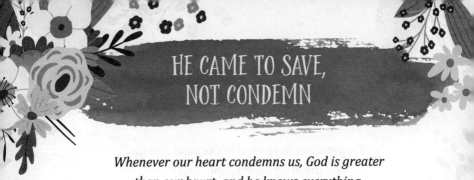

HE CAME TO SAVE, NOT CONDEMN

Whenever our heart condemns us, God is greater than our heart, and he knows everything.
1 JOHN 3:20 ESV

You've tried to let it go, but it's driving you crazy. That thing you did. . . you can't stop thinking about it. Yes, you've already confessed it. Yes, Jesus has forgiven you. The people you've hurt are working hard to forgive you too. But you're having a hard time forgiving yourself. How did you mess up like that? You knew better.

Guilt is a tricky thing. It wraps its tentacles around you and tries to keep you from moving forward. But here's the truth: if you've truly asked God to forgive you for what you did, and if you're making an effort to make things right with the people you hurt, you have to forgive yourself.

That's easier said than done, for sure. But you have to try. Don't let the enemy consume your thoughts with negative self-chatter. It's so pointless, and it weighs you down. Instead, proclaim, "I'm set free from that!" as you move forward. God has a lot for you to do. So no self-condemnation, girl.

It's hard, Jesus, but I'll do my best to forgive myself. I'm truly sorry for what I did. Help me do better next time. Amen.

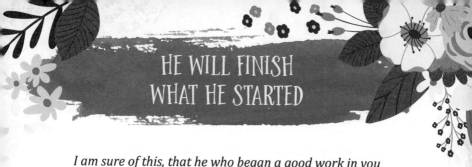

HE WILL FINISH WHAT HE STARTED

I am sure of this, that he who began a good work in you will bring it to completion at the day of Jesus Christ.
PHILIPPIANS 1:6 ESV

You started that art project for your room. . .but didn't finish it.

You started a diary. . .but forgot about it.

You started keeping your room organized on January 1. . .then got sloppy again.

Girl, you've sure started a lot of things!

Aren't you glad God isn't like you? When He starts something (like the work He did on the cross), He follows through. He's never waiting to "get around to that." In the blink of an eye, He's already done it! He's fulfilled His promise.

He began a good work in you, and He has promised to see it through. He won't leave you hanging. And because you're created in His image, you can live this way too. (Hey, a girl of value places value in being like her heavenly Father!)

Finish what you start. It's a great way to live and a terrific opportunity to be more like Christ.

I get it, Lord. I need to do a better job of carrying through. Make me more like You in this way, I pray. Amen.

HIS FACE IN THE MIRROR

All of us, with no covering on our faces, show the shining-greatness of the Lord as in a mirror. All the time we are being changed to look like Him, with more and more of His shining-greatness. This change is from the Lord Who is the Spirit.
2 Corinthians 3:18 nlv

You look at your reflection in the mirror and groan. The past few days have been really hard on you. It started with a mess-up on your end. That led to a misunderstanding between friends. That led to a break in a relationship. Now things are a hot mess, and you wonder if they can be fixed. Your eyes look tired. Your smile is gone. The face staring back at you looks defeated.

Girl, it's time to catch a glimpse of today's verse. No matter what you've done, you can ask for (and receive) forgiveness. When that happens, the shining-greatness of the Lord greets you in the mirror. Instead of seeing defeat, you see hope for restored relationships. Instead of hiding away from the world, the veil is gone, and you're happy to get back out there among people again.

You're looking more and more like Him every time you say, "I am so sorry, Jesus! I really messed that up." That's all He's looking for, after all—a heart that wants to make Him happy.

I did mess up, Jesus. And I don't like the way things look right now. I ask for Your forgiveness so that I can start over again. Amen.

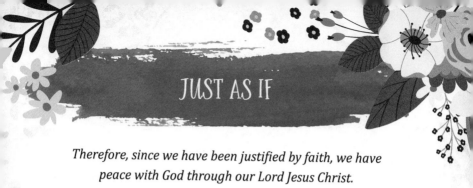

JUST AS IF

Therefore, since we have been justified by faith, we have peace with God through our Lord Jesus Christ.
ROMANS 5:1 ESV

Take a close look at today's verse. Do you know what the word *justified* means? To be justified means it's "just as if" you never sinned in the first place, like it never even happened.

Whoa. Is God really that good, or is He just forgetful? Doesn't He remember the pain you caused?

The Bible says that God tosses your sin as far as the east is from the west. He remembers it no more (unless you keep reminding Him, which isn't a great idea). He truly wants you to get past it and move on.

You might have some work to do in relationships that you've damaged, but when it comes to your relationship with your heavenly Father, He sees you as forgiven. Just as if you didn't mess up in the first place.

What a remarkable, loving God. He finds you worthy of His love—no matter what!

I don't know how You do it, Lord! You forgive. . .and forget. It's amazing. I'm so grateful for second chances! Amen.

IT ISN'T CLEAR YET

Dear friends, now we are God's children. What we will be isn't completely clear yet. We do know that when Christ appears we will be like him because we will see him as he is. So all people who have this confidence in Christ keep themselves pure, as Christ is pure.

1 JOHN 3:2–3 GW

Sometimes, like today's verse says, things just aren't clear yet. You wish you could see the road ahead, but there's a thick fog hanging overhead, and you're just not sure.

Imagine you're getting ready for school and you need to fix your hair and put on some makeup. You go to the bathroom mirror, but steam from the shower you took earlier has clouded it over. What do you do? You take your hand and swipe it across the mirror to clear the image.

Don't you wish you could do that with God? Don't you wish He would reveal everything all at once? (Have you ever wondered why He doesn't?)

He loves you, girl. And He wants you to know that, little by little, you're becoming more like Him. It's not going to happen overnight. But with every right choice you make, the image in the mirror becomes clearer. The fog on the road lifts. You're on the path to holiness, and it's looking good on you, girl!

I make mistakes, Lord. You keep forgiving me and giving me second chances. I know You're doing a work in me. I can feel it! One day I'll see it all clearly. Until then, I will trust You! Amen.

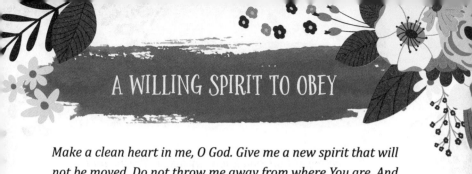

A WILLING SPIRIT TO OBEY

Make a clean heart in me, O God. Give me a new spirit that will not be moved. Do not throw me away from where You are. And do not take Your Holy Spirit from me. Let the joy of Your saving power return to me. And give me a willing spirit to obey you.
PSALM 51:10–12 NLV

Have you ever obeyed someone because you had no other choice? Maybe your heart wasn't in it, but what could you do? You had to take that test. You had to turn in that assignment. You had to babysit your kid brother. You had no other options.

Doing something grudgingly isn't the same as doing it with a willing and excited heart, is it? It's boring. Mundane. Not adventurous.

Today's verse from Psalm 51 says that God can return "a willing spirit" to obey. Wow. You can actually ask for more of the zeal to enjoy obedience. (Cool thought, right?)

Is there a certain adult you struggle to obey? If so, then focus your prayers on him or her. Ask God to give you a clean heart. Confess any bitterness you've held toward that person. Then ask Him to give you a new spirit, a new outlook. (He'll do it if you ask!) Before long, you can obey with a happy heart.

I come to You today, Jesus, and confess that I have a hard time obeying _____. Help me, I pray! Amen.

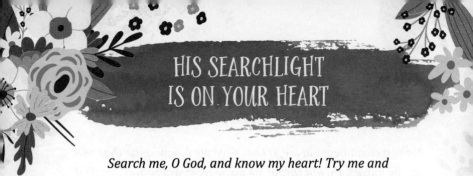

HIS SEARCHLIGHT IS ON YOUR HEART

Search me, O God, and know my heart! Try me and know my thoughts! And see if there be any grievous way in me, and lead me in the way everlasting!
PSALM 139:23–24 ESV

Have you ever heard the expression, "You can run, but you can't hide!"? It's true. God will always find you out. And just because you haven't shared something openly with a friend or loved one doesn't mean no one knows it. God searches your heart and sees all.

Maybe that idea creeps you out. You kind of wish God couldn't see inside your heart. After all, you've had some not-so-nice thoughts go through there. Some ugliness has taken up residence in your heart's chambers over the years.

God is searching, like a janitor with a broom in hand. He wants to sweep out the cobwebs, the dust bunnies. If He finds anything that might cause trouble, He sweeps it up, bit by bit. He won't leave anything behind.

Why? Because He adores you. He wants His girls to have clean hands and pure hearts! He wants to set you free from the pain of hanging on to the icky stuff. He's a Master Cleaner. No doubt about it!

Come on in and clean up, Jesus! I'm ready. Amen.

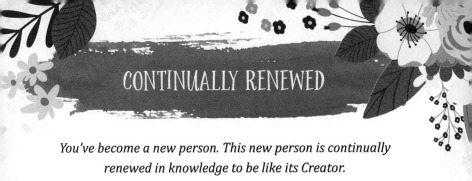

CONTINUALLY RENEWED

You've become a new person. This new person is continually renewed in knowledge to be like its Creator.
COLOSSIANS 3:10 GW

Have you ever had a subscription to a magazine? They can be fun, but if you're not careful, the magazine company might set you up for an automatic renewal. That means they can charge your bank account every year, without your knowledge, so that you go on receiving new editions—whether you want them or not!

God has an automatic renewal policy too! He's making everything inside of you new. And tomorrow it'll be new again. And the day after that too. Every day, He renews your life. He zaps you with fresh starts, new energy, new excitement to face the tasks ahead.

Today's verse from Colossians explains that you've become a new person. You're continually being renewed to be more like Jesus. Every minute of every hour of every day of every year. You're becoming more like Him. . .in increments!

Sure, you wish it could happen all at once, but here's the cool part: you're on a journey! And every day is an adventure as you become more like your heavenly Father.

Thanks for taking me on the journey, Jesus!
I want to be more like You. Amen.

DO YOUR BEST

Do your best to know that God is pleased with you.
Be as a workman who has nothing to be ashamed
of. Teach the words of truth in the right way.
2 Timothy 2:15 nlv

It might be easy to read all of these devotions about how God calls you worthy and think that you can live however you want. Some girls do that—even Christian girls. They say, "God will forgive me, so why not sneak in a few things that I shouldn't?"

There are a thousand reasons why you shouldn't, but the number one reason is because it breaks God's heart. Your heavenly Father really truly wants you to try your best. Be a worker who has nothing to be ashamed of.

Think about that for a minute. If you were in construction work and were asked to build a house, would you use shoddy materials? Would you leave the framework of the house half-finished and sheetrock over it? Of course not! You would do your best work, or a strong wind would blow the house down and reveal your sloppiness!

Don't build a weak frame in your relationship with Jesus. Live the right way. You'll make Him proud, and you will have the satisfaction of knowing you did your best.

I'll do my best, Jesus! No sloppy work here! Amen.

HE'S LOOKING FOR
AN "I'M SORRY!"

"I tell you, there will be more joy in heaven because of one sinner who is sorry for his sins and turns from them, than for ninety-nine people right with God who do not have sins to be sorry for."
LUKE 15:7 NLV

Did you realize that the angels in heaven throw a party when you admit you've messed up? Might sound extreme, but that's pretty much what happens! Today's verse says that there's more joy in heaven over one sinner who's sorry for her sins (and actually leaves them behind) than for all the people who never sinned in the first place. Whoa!

Why do you think God feels so strongly about repentance? (By the way, *repentance* is just a fancy word that means "turning away from sin.") He wants you to acknowledge when you've done something wrong. He doesn't want you to sweep it under the rug or pretend you're not to blame when you really are.

If you really want to start a party in heaven today, spend some time admitting what you've been up to, girl. It's not like God doesn't know anyway. But then turn away from that stuff and commit to never do it again!

*Lord, I have some things on my heart today
I need to share with You. Amen.*

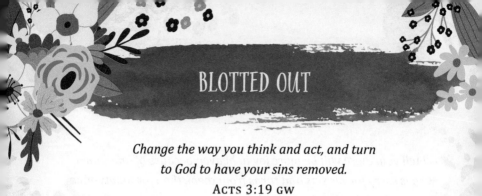

BLOTTED OUT

Change the way you think and act, and turn
to God to have your sins removed.
ACTS 3:19 GW

Picture an artist working on a painting. He's almost done when he accidentally spills a can of paint across his canvas. His whole painting is now buried under the big blob. Awful!

When something is covered by something else, you can't see what was there originally. That's how it is when your sins are covered by the blood of Jesus. You can't see them, and He can't see them either! They've been blotted out.

You have to trust Jesus' work on the cross, girl. When you feel like your sins are still there, trust Him that they're gone. And while you're at it, go ahead and change the way you think and act. This is an important part of the equation. It wouldn't make sense to keep coming back to Him for a repeat performance of the same sin. (How awkward would that be?)

Let Him blot out your sin once and for all. When it's gone, you'll have a fresh start, an amazing do-over. That's how much He loves you, girl!

Thank You for blotting out my sin, Jesus! It's
washed away, never to be seen again. Help me
live a life that's pleasing to You. Amen.

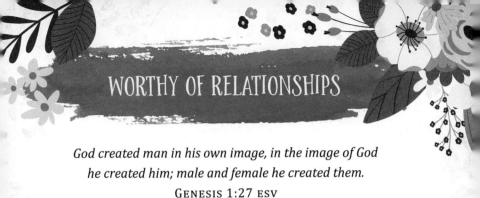

WORTHY OF RELATIONSHIPS

God created man in his own image, in the image of God
he created him; male and female he created them.
GENESIS 1:27 ESV

When you struggle with feelings of unworthiness, it's not always easy to imagine that you will have good relationships with others. You might even find yourself wondering why others would want to hang out with you. After all, you are so messed up. You are so flawed. (Or so you think!)

Girl, that's exactly what the enemy wants you to believe. But God says otherwise. He believes that you are worthy of relationships. If He didn't, then why would He want to be in relationship with you? The God of the universe adores you, wants to spend time with you, and thinks that you are worth hanging out with.

You are, you know. You are precious—not just in His sight, but to those who take the time to know you. They will think you're worthy of relationships too once they get to know you. So brace yourself! There are lots of relationships ahead.

Thank You for thinking I'm worth hanging
out with, Lord. That makes me feel so good!
May I make others feel like that. Amen.

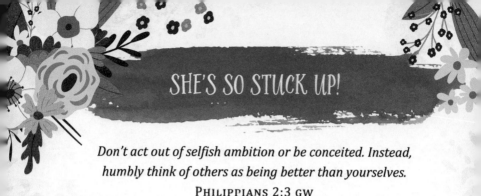

*Don't act out of selfish ambition or be conceited. Instead,
humbly think of others as being better than yourselves.*
PHILIPPIANS 2:3 GW

You've met them—those girls who are so stuck up they could drown in a rainstorm. They think they're "all that," and it shows in everything they do. Unfortunately, they usually have a group of girls around them who cheer them on. Ugh.

You, though? You're not conceited. You learned when you gave your heart to Jesus that living for Him is better than living for yourself. So you do your best not to live a selfish, me-focused life. In fact, you're learning that being others-focused is a great way to live. (Hey, it relieves the pressure of always having to appear perfect!)

You're on the right track, girl. So don't worry about the ones who are stuck up. The world will figure out that they're not as perfect as they say they are. That's between them and God, anyway. You just go on doing what you know to do, and He will give you amazing friends who think you're awesome!

Thanks for making me others-focused, Jesus. I don't want to be a me, myself, and I girl anymore. Amen.

LET'S GIVE 'EM A HAND, FOLKS!

Let us help each other to love others and to do good. Let us not stay away from church meetings. Some people are doing this all the time. Comfort each other as you see the day of His return coming near.

HEBREWS 10:24–25 NLV

Human beings are weird. We love it when we get pats on the back, but we're not as keen to see others get applause. Why is that?

Maybe your friend has graduated at the top of her class. You want to cheer her on, but you're a little jealous. Your name is way down on the class list. Oh, you smile and pretend to be happy for her, but inside you're really just jealous.

Sound familiar? We struggle with things like this, don't we?

It's time to give those friends and loved ones a little credit, girl! They need encouragement just like you do. Stick together. Be a team. Be their biggest cheerleader, in fact. But don't fake it. Really mean it!

You might have to ask Jesus for help to really mean it, but that's okay. He's had bigger issues to fix before. Just be real with Him, and He'll get it straightened out.

Jesus, if I'm really honest with You, I don't always feel like being a cheerleader for others. I'm definitely going to need Your help with this one! Amen.

LIVE IN HARMONY

*May God, who gives you this endurance and encouragement,
allow you to live in harmony with each other by
following the example of Christ Jesus.*

ROMANS 15:5 GW

God believes you're worthy of relationships, but He's hoping they will be good ones! In order to build a strong relational foundation, you've got to strive for one very important thing: harmony.

What's harmony, you ask? Well, think of it like this. When you go to see a play, you hear the orchestra warming up just ahead of time. All the instruments play random notes on top of one another. It sounds awful! But then, when the play begins, they're suddenly all in harmony. That's because they're all playing from the same musical sheet. They're following the score. They're working together.

God wants His kids to work together too. Don't fight and bicker. Don't squabble over senseless things. It's not worth it (and, frankly, it gives God a bad name when His kids embarrass Him like that). Live together like a wonderful melodic song!

*I'll do my best to live in harmony with people, Jesus.
It's tempting to sing my own notes, especially when I'm
angry, but I'll stick to Your musical plan! Amen.*

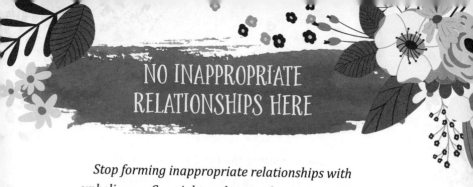

NO INAPPROPRIATE RELATIONSHIPS HERE

Stop forming inappropriate relationships with unbelievers. Can right and wrong be partners? Can light have anything in common with darkness?
2 CORINTHIANS 6:14 GW

Can right and wrong be partners? Pause to think about that question. It's an important one, especially when it comes to who you hang out with.

So who do you spend time with? You don't really get a lot of say over who sits next to you in class. But when it comes to who you hang out with after school, who you confide in, who you go to the movies with? Yeah, you get to pick. So pick wisely.

You want to be a good witness to your friends, of course. And you might argue, "Isn't the point to lead people to Christ?" Yes. Right. But that doesn't mean you pull just anyone into your inner circle, especially if being around them is going to tempt you toward wrong living.

Tread carefully, girl. You want to keep a good balance between pleasing God and being a witness to others. You know your limits. Guard yourself accordingly!

I'll be careful, Lord! I want to be a witness, but I know there are certain people I can't really link arms with. Give me courage to say no to them. Amen.

MOMS AND DADS

Children, obey your parents in the Lord, for this is right. "Honor your father and mother" (this is the first commandment with a promise), "that it may go well with you and that you may live long in the land."

Ephesians 6:1–3 esv

You want things to go well in your life, right? Well, here's a biblical promise to guarantee that: honor your mother and father. It makes God's heart happy when you get this relationship right. Sure, there might be issues. There might be ups and downs. But there's a promise associated with this commandment. When you obey your parents, God makes an actual promise that things will go well with you and you'll live long in the land.

Wow! *Well, when You put it like that, Lord!* It makes you want to work harder on those parental relationships, doesn't it? He cares so much about this particular relationship, because your parents are a representation (on earth) of your Father in heaven. This doesn't mean they always get it right, but they command a certain level of respect, simply because they're your authority figures.

Honor your parents, girl. You want to get this one right!

I'll do my best, Lord. I don't always try very hard, but I will do better. Amen.

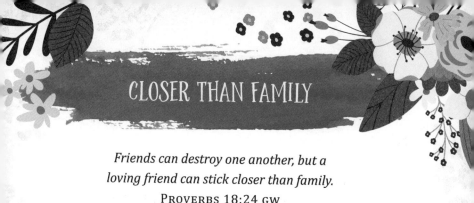

CLOSER THAN FAMILY

Friends can destroy one another, but a
loving friend can stick closer than family.
PROVERBS 18:24 GW

You know what it's like to have volatile relationships with friends. Some are *h-a-r-d*. They make your life very difficult. Others, though? They're just like family. You know the ones. They stick closer than glue. You couldn't shake them if you wanted to. In fact, some of them are even closer than your own family. You didn't plan it that way. It just happened.

Why do you suppose God gives you friendships like this? He knows you need them! The more tight, close relationships, the better! Family's got your back, girl! They know your deepest, darkest secrets and love you anyway. These close friends do too.

So honor them as you honor your family. Hang tight. Be there for them like they're there for you. God thinks you're special enough that He's blessed you with an extra sister (or brother). He's good like that!

I'm so grateful for the ones who are like family,
Jesus! I can't shake them. . .but I wouldn't want
to! Thanks for sending them my way. Amen.

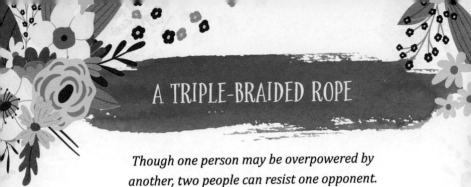

A TRIPLE-BRAIDED ROPE

*Though one person may be overpowered by
another, two people can resist one opponent.
A triple-braided rope is not easily broken.*
ECCLESIASTES 4:12 GW

If you've ever braided your hair, you know the process of taking three strands and braiding them together into one. The result is thicker. Stronger.

Now imagine you're doing that with three ropes. Let's say you need to tether a boat to a dock. One rope won't do it. Two won't be strong enough. But as soon as you take three ropes and braid them, you've got a rope that can take a *l-o-t* of pressure.

Your friendships can be like that rope. When you're "tight" with a friend, you're invincible. Let those enemies try to take you down! You're braided to your friend, and now you're a force to be reckoned with.

Which friendships are like this in your life? Who's got your back? Who can you count on in a crisis? Today, take the time to thank God for braiding your life together with those people. What a gift they are!

*Thanks for my braided friendships, Jesus.
You must care a lot about me to give me
friends who have my back! Amen.*

PUT ON LOVE

*Above all these put on love, which binds
everything together in perfect harmony.*
COLOSSIANS 3:14 ESV

When a quilter gets ready to "bind" a quilt, she takes a long piece of fabric and sews it to the outside edges of the quilt on all sides. The binding holds all of the other pieces together. Without it, those fabric blocks wouldn't look right.

Chefs use binders too. When baking cookies or cakes, they often use eggs to hold the other ingredients together. Skip the binder and your sweets won't bake up the same. (Try it and see!)

What is the great "binder" that Jesus recommends? Love, of course! When all else fails, love succeeds. It's the fabric holding the quilt of life together. It's the missing ingredient when you're baking up a new relationship. When you "put on" love, everything holds together in perfect harmony. Your heavenly Father knows an amazing secret—love really does hold all things together.

I get it, Lord. When I love like You do, all areas of my life come together seamlessly. Thank You for showing me how to put it on. Amen.

THE GOLDEN RULE

"In everything, do to others what you would have them do to you, for this sums up the Law and the Prophets."
MATTHEW 7:12 NIV

God has blessed you above and beyond what you deserve. You sense it and you're grateful. He's also given you terrific advice for how to live in this world. Great advice. Life-changing advice. And when it comes to your relationships, He's given you a particular nugget from His Word that will (literally) fix any problem you could face. We call it the "Golden Rule," and it goes like this: Do unto others as you would have others do unto you.

That's it! Treat others the way you want to be treated. Not the way you have been treated in the past. Not the way you're currently being treated. Instead, Jesus wants you to treat others your absolute best, even if they treat you the absolute worst.

Ouch! This isn't easy. In fact, it might be the hardest thing He asks you to do. But God knows a secret: if even one person in a relationship is willing to make a move in the right direction, there is a greater chance for healing and restoration. And that's what you ultimately want, right?

Lord, it's not going to be easy, but I do know how I would like to be treated, so I'll start there. I'll treat the other person that way and trust You to work out the problems. Amen.

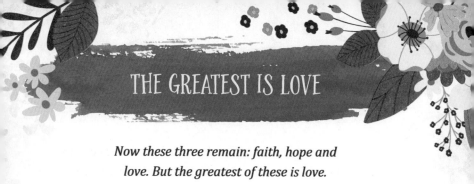

THE GREATEST IS LOVE

Now these three remain: faith, hope and
love. But the greatest of these is love.
1 CORINTHIANS 13:13 NIV

Because God sees you as His worthy child, He's poured out awesome gifts on you. (Hey, if He didn't think you deserved them, He wouldn't lavish them on you!)

You've been blessed with amazing relationships and many other blessings besides! He's taken care of your needs from the time you arrived on the planet until now, and He doesn't plan to stop anytime soon. But if you took every single thing He's ever given you—*every single one*—there would be *one* that would sit at the top of the list.

Love.

Love trumps everything. Literally, everything. It trumps joy. It trumps hope. It trumps financial blessings, healings, and anything else you could imagine. Why is love the most valuable of all the gifts? Because it was love that sent Jesus to the cross. It was love that convinced Him to come as a babe in a manger. It was love that caused Him to lay down His life for you. If not for love, none of the other gifts would bring fulfillment or peace. Everything else hangs on this one word: love.

I get it, Jesus. You gave the greatest gift when You gave Yourself. Nothing else even comes close. I'm so grateful! Amen.

TWO ARE BETTER THAN ONE

*Two people are better than one because together they have
a good reward for their hard work. If one falls, the other can
help his friend get up. But how tragic it is for the one who is
all alone when he falls. There is no one to help him get up.*

ECCLESIASTES 4:9–10 GW

"There's strength in numbers." No doubt you've heard that phrase. But it's so true, especially when you're talking about people.

Picture this: you're traveling down a road all alone in your car. The front left tire blows out. You manage to get the car pulled off the road, but you're feeling upset and confused. You want to call someone but can't wrap your thoughts around who you should call first.

Now imagine that same scenario but with another person in the car. No doubt she would jump right in and calm you down, then take your phone and make the call for you. She might even get out and change the tire!

Two are better than one. If you fall, she'll help you up. If you have a task to complete, she'll help you get it done in half the time.

There really is strength in numbers, girl!

*God, thank You for my friendships!
I place value in my friends, Lord. Amen.*

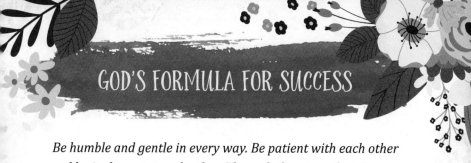

GOD'S FORMULA FOR SUCCESS

Be humble and gentle in every way. Be patient with each other and lovingly accept each other. Through the peace that ties you together, do your best to maintain the unity that the Spirit gives.
EPHESIANS 4:2–3 GW

If God had a magic formula for success, Ephesians 4:2–3 might be it! Can you imagine how transformed the world would be if everyone followed this simple advice?

Be humble. Let's stop right there. Being humble means you have to lay down your pride. That's not easy to do!

Be gentle in every way. *Every way, Lord? Really?*

Be patient with each other. Ouch. Patience is easier said than done, right?

Lovingly accept each other. Hang on a minute! We're all really different. We *really* have to accept each other?

Maintain unity through peace. Act like we all get along, even when things are rough? How does that work?

Oh, but if we tried, if we really laid down pride and treated others with this kind of love, what a wonderful, wonderful world it would be!

Lord You say I'm worthy of friendships, and I'm so glad. But I want to make the most of them. Help me follow this formula for success, I pray! Amen.

LET YOUR LIGHT SHINE

"In the same way, let your light shine before others,
so that they may see your good works and give
glory to your Father who is in heaven."
MATTHEW 5:16 ESV

God says, "Let your light shine." But what does that mean exactly?

Think of it this way: God is shining bright like the sun. You are meant to be a reflection of Him to this (very) lost world. When friends look at you, they should see Him.

Instead of snapping at people, respond in love.

Instead of growing impatient with people, take a deep breath and give them more time.

Instead of griping and complaining, figure out new ways to bless people.

It's really that easy. Love them the way He loves them. In doing so, you're shining His light so brightly that others can't help but notice. But remember, it's not really you they're noticing. Oh, they might see your good deeds, but the whole point is to guide them straight to Him.

Jesus, I want to shine bright for You. You alone are worthy
of praise. Nothing I do can ever come close, but I want to
be a shining example to point everyone to You. Amen.

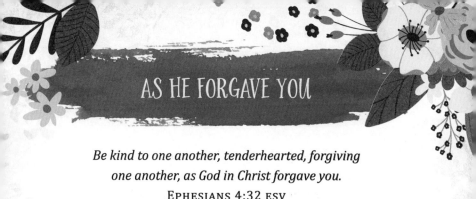

AS HE FORGAVE YOU

Be kind to one another, tenderhearted, forgiving
one another, as God in Christ forgave you.
EPHESIANS 4:32 ESV

If someone asked you to make a list of all the things God has forgiven you for, would it be a long list? What would you add to it? Jealousy? Cheating? Lying? Anger?

Here's the deal—in spite of your past sins, Jesus says you're worthy because you're His child. But you haven't always made His job easy, girl! There have been plenty of mess-ups, things He's had to forgive.

Now think about that person who grates on your nerves. You know the one. She annoys you to no end. She wears you out. You've lost patience with her. Then you read this verse from Ephesians 4:32 and you realize that God is asking you to be as patient with her as He has been with you.

Wait a minute. . .is that even fair?

Yes. Yes, it is. God has been so gracious, loving, and tenderhearted with you. How could you be anything other than that to the people you know?

I'll try harder to be patient with others, Jesus,
and to forgive them when they hurt me.
You do that for me, after all. Amen.

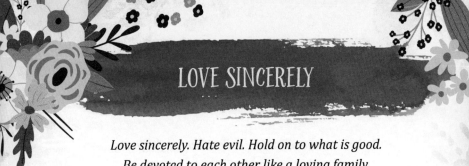

LOVE SINCERELY

Love sincerely. Hate evil. Hold on to what is good.
Be devoted to each other like a loving family.
Excel in showing respect for each other.
ROMANS 12:9–10 GW

You are worthy of God's love. Think about that for a moment. The Creator of the universe took the time to fall in love with you. He thinks you're amazing. And He's hoping that same love He's feeling for you will be shared with others.

Take a look at today's verse. God doesn't just want you to love—He wants you to love sincerely. Honestly. Deeply. Truly. The kind of love this verse refers to is devotion, like a parent would have to a child or a husband and wife would have for each other. When you're devoted, you're in it for the long haul.

God is in this for the long haul with you, and He's hoping you'll extend that same commitment to those you love. Hang tight to them. Treat them like family. Show respect. If you do all of these things, you'll have friendships that last for years.

Lord, I want to love the way You love. I want to be devoted as You're devoted. May I be more like You in every way, Jesus. Amen.

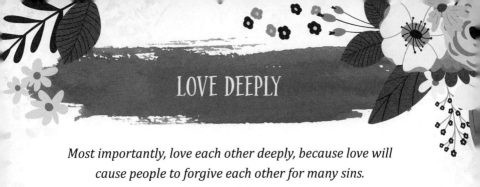

LOVE DEEPLY

Most importantly, love each other deeply, because love will cause people to forgive each other for many sins.
1 Peter 4:8 ncv

Have you ever been in love? Oh, maybe you've had a crush on someone, but have you experienced that heart-pounding, pulse-racing love that everyone talks about? If not, you will! No doubt soon.

There are so many different kinds of love—from the romantic version to the kind of love that friends share. Then, of course, there's agape love, which is the love between God and man.

No matter who you're loving, one thing is clear from today's verse: God wants your love to run deep. Think of it like the root of a tree. If those roots don't go down deep, then a strong wind can come along and flip that tree over!

Relationships will flip over if the roots aren't deep too, so make up your mind to do the hard work to make those friendships grow. They will stand the test of time if the roots run deep.

Lord, thank You for saying that relationships have value and worth! I'm so glad to be surrounded by loving, caring people. Our roots run deep, Jesus! Amen.

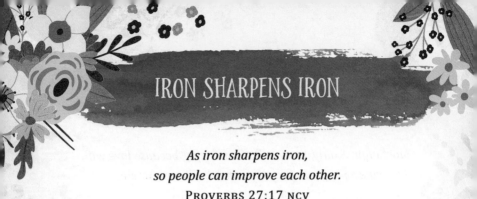

IRON SHARPENS IRON

As iron sharpens iron,
so people can improve each other.
PROVERBS 27:17 NCV

Have you ever tried to cut something with a dull knife? It can be a real pain. Unless that knife is sharpened, it's almost useless. And let's face it, the harder you have to work a knife, the more potential for disaster!

Now compare that dull knife to your relationships. Some are like that, aren't they? You have to work really hard at them. They're difficult. Hard to manage.

Others, though? They're sharp. They work beautifully.

Here's a really cool truth found in today's verse: we're all like knives in need of sharpening. And God intends for our friendships to serve as tools to keep us sharp. If you're hanging out with spiritually dull people, they won't sharpen you. You might want to give that some serious thought! Hanging out with sharp people means they make you better as you spend time together. This is the way God intends for it to work. Iron sharpens iron, girl. People who are strong in their faith will rub off on you (and vice versa)!

I get it, Jesus. I'll be one sharp knife if I hang out with believers who are spiritually strong!

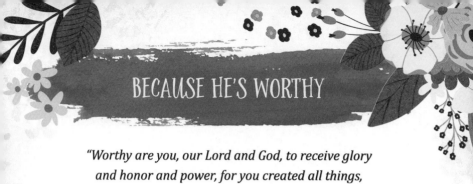

BECAUSE HE'S WORTHY

*"Worthy are you, our Lord and God, to receive glory
and honor and power, for you created all things,
and by your will they existed and were created."*
REVELATION 4:11 ESV

God calls you worthy, but by now you've figured out that He's truly the only One who's really worthy. It's only because of His worthiness that you have value and worth in the first place. Revelation 4:11 says "Worthy are you, our Lord and God, to receive glory and honor and power."

There's coming a day when we will gather around His throne and cry out, "Holy, holy, holy is the Lord God Almighty!" No one else you know will ever receive such praise. Many people have been made worthy by the blood of Jesus, but He's the only One who will get our total adoration.

Why? Because He created everything! He's the ultimate Author of all. Everything that was, everything that is, everything that will ever be is only because of Him. He alone is God. And for that reason, He alone is worthy of our eternal praise.

Lord, thank You for dying and making me worthy, but I get it! You're the only One truly worthy, Jesus. Amen.

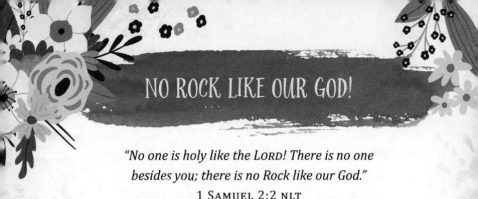

NO ROCK LIKE OUR GOD!

"No one is holy like the LORD! There is no one besides you; there is no Rock like our God."
1 SAMUEL 2:2 NLT

No one compares to God. No king. No president. No pastor. No actor. No politician. No billionaire. Absolutely no one on planet earth who ever lived or who will ever live in the future can even come close.

Can any of them bring about world peace? Can any of them claim to save others? Can any say that they are truly holy? Absolutely not!

Can any of them provide comfort and shelter like God can? Can any of them remain steady as a rock when the world is shaking? Can any of those people rise from the dead? Definitely not!

There is no one like our God. He's worthy of your praise, no matter what you're facing. He alone is the Savior who gave His life for you. He'd do it again too if He had to. Who else would do that for you, girl?

No one but your Rock, Jesus. He is above all, in all, and through all. . . and yet He would drop everything in an instant just to be with you.

Thank You, Jesus! You stand alone.
No one is holy like You. Amen.

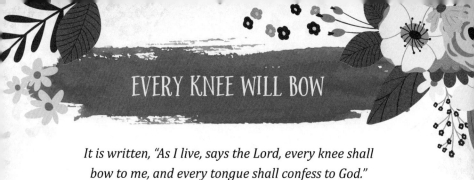

EVERY KNEE WILL BOW

It is written, "As I live, says the Lord, every knee shall bow to me, and every tongue shall confess to God."
ROMANS 14:11 ESV

There's coming a day when every knee will bow and every tongue will confess that Jesus Christ is Lord. Stop to think about that for a moment. That person you know who's an atheist? She will one day bow the knee. That person on TV who makes such a big deal out of making fun of Christians? He will have to answer to God too. Those people who persecute Christians, even putting them to death? They will stand before the King of kings to give an account of what they've done. Even they will have to acknowledge that He is God.

Every knee will bow. People from every nation and tribe. Every tongue will confess in every language known to mankind, from the beginning of time until now. And when that great day comes, there will be no lingering doubts. All of humanity will have to acknowledge that God really is who He says He is and that He is Lord of all.

Lord, I'm looking forward to the day when every knee bows and every tongue confesses that You are God! Amen.

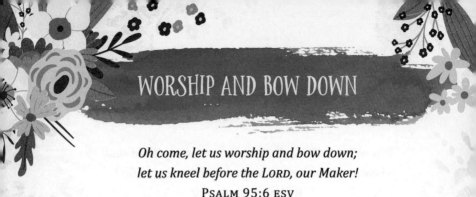

WORSHIP AND BOW DOWN

Oh come, let us worship and bow down;
let us kneel before the LORD, our Maker!
PSALM 95:6 ESV

Picture a toy maker in a workshop. He's made rows and rows of dolls. Some have curly blond hair. Others have dark, wavy hair. He's crafted them in every skin tone, every shape, every size. They sit on the shelves, waiting to be sold to girls and boys. Can those dolls ever thank their maker? Nope! They're lifeless beings, simple creations meant to entertain kids, but no more.

Now think about your Maker, God. He crafted human beings in His own image. You're very much like Him! And one of the key things you have in common with your Creator is His Spirit, which lives inside of you. (Hey, no doll can claim that!) You're a "house" for His Spirit. (Cool, right?)

Dolls will never bow down and praise the doll maker. But you, girl? You can bow down every day to thank your heavenly Father for creating you, for loving you, for finding you worthy through the sacrifice of His Son.

Come! Kneel down! Bow before the Lord (either literally or symbolically), and thank Him for giving you life.

I'm so grateful, Lord! My heart is humbled as I come into Your presence! One day I'll gather with all of mankind to sing Your praises. Amen!

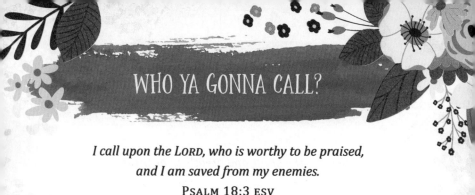

WHO YA GONNA CALL?

I call upon the LORD, who is worthy to be praised,
and I am saved from my enemies.
PSALM 18:3 ESV

Who do you call when you're in trouble? What's the first number you punch into your phone when you're in crisis mode? Your dad? Your mom? Your best friend? A leader from your church? No doubt a name came to mind right away as you read that question. You've got a short list of people you could count on to rescue you.

Here's a fun fact: God wants to be your first call. He wants you to remember that He alone is worthy. So call on Him. Cry out His name. He will sweep in and rescue you. He'll save you from your enemies. (Could anyone else do that? No way!)

His capabilities are so far beyond that of mere humans. Some people will come to your rescue in a pinch or offer great advice. But when it comes to the big stuff? Only God is able. Only God is willing. Only God is worthy.

Run to Him, girl. He's waiting with open arms.

I'm coming straight to You, Lord! You're my
first call, and not just when I'm in trouble!
I'm so honored to be Your kid! Amen.

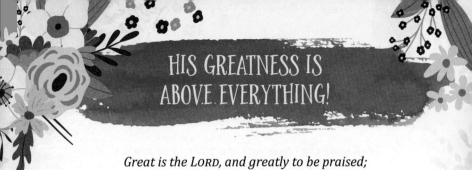

HIS GREATNESS IS ABOVE EVERYTHING!

Great is the LORD, and greatly to be praised;
and his greatness is unsearchable.

PSALM 145:3 KJV

God's greatness is unsearchable. What images come to mind as you read those words? He's above and beyond anything and everything, too lofty for you to even comprehend!

Think about this: there's no mountain high enough to top Him. There's no movie star famous enough to outshine Him. There's no athlete amazing enough to outrace Him. There's no river mighty enough to wash Him away. He's greater than all of those things.

Your amazing heavenly Father is worthy of your praise simply for who He is. He's the Almighty Author of everything, the One who hung the stars out in space. The One who thought that tadpoles should one day become frogs. The One who decided that zebras should have stripes.

He's more brilliant than all of the scientists put together, more compassionate than the kindest grandmother, and more loving than the most romantic movie hero.

He's God. And He's dying for a relationship with you.

No, really. He died for a relationship with you, His worthy child.

Lord, You're above all! I give You praise! Thank You for loving me and finding me worthy. Amen.

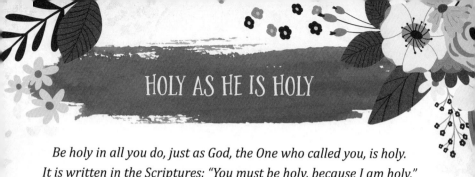

HOLY AS HE IS HOLY

Be holy in all you do, just as God, the One who called you, is holy.
It is written in the Scriptures: "You must be holy, because I am holy."
1 PETER 1:15–16 NCV

When Jesus said, "Be holy, because I am holy," do you think He actually meant that you should be perfect? He is, after all. And His version of holiness is pure perfection.

Here's the truth: Jesus knows that you'll never be perfect in this lifetime, but He wants you to aspire to it. (Hey, if you don't set goals, you'll never reach them!) He's telling you, *"Try harder. Be more like Me. Climb higher. Reach further. Do more. Be better. Stretch yourself!"*

You *can* be more like Jesus. You really can. In the way you speak to others. In how you treat your family. In how you handle yourself with friends and teachers at school. These are all ways to try.

When you strive to be like the most holy, worthy Creator, you become a better version of yourself. And that's the goal, isn't it? So try, girl. Really try.

Jesus, I want to be more like You. Make me holy as You are holy, I pray. Amen.

HE ALONE IS WORTHY

They sang a new song, saying, "Worthy are you to take the scroll and to open its seals, for you were slain, and by your blood you ransomed people for God from every tribe and language and people and nation."
REVELATION 5:9 ESV

There's coming a day when death and sadness will end, when we'll all be safely in heaven with the One who created us. And when we're there, we'll see—once and for all—that the price Jesus paid on the cross was worth it for all of mankind.

Today's verse gives us a glimpse into a story that will one day come to pass. Jesus, the spotless Lamb, will be given a scroll to open. And, as He opens it, all in attendance will be absolutely sure of one thing: only *He* is worthy to open it. None of them are able, but Jesus is! Only He is sinless, spotless, holy. And because of who He is, He's given sole permission to do what no one else can do.

Think of a jailer with a key to the cell. He's the only one trusted to keep it. Jesus is like that jailer, holding the keys in His hand. And He uses them to unlock the doors to our hearts.

Jesus, You alone are worthy! No one even comes close. I worship You for who You are! Amen.

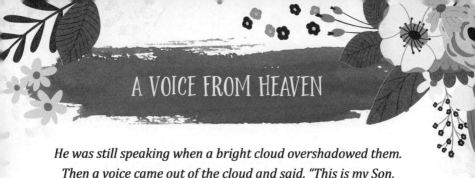

A VOICE FROM HEAVEN

He was still speaking when a bright cloud overshadowed them.
Then a voice came out of the cloud and said, "This is my Son,
whom I love and with whom I am pleased. Listen to him!"
MATTHEW 17:5 GW

One of the first indicators that Jesus really was who He said He was came on the day He was baptized by John the Baptist. When He came up out of the water, a voice from heaven came out of a cloud and spoke over the group that had gathered there: *"This is my Son, whom I love and with whom I am pleased. Listen to him!"*

Whoa. Imagine if you had been in the crowd that day. How startling that must have been! And yet, how convincing! You would never doubt that Jesus was the Savior of the world if His own Dad spoke up and told you so, after all.

Jesus got a great endorsement that day. And guess what? God's given you an endorsement too! He says that you are worthy because the Savior (His Son) died on the cross for you. So, in a way, that proclamation from heaven included you too!

Cool, right?

I get it, Lord! When You said You were well pleased with Your Son, You knew that He would one day die on the cross for me. I'm so grateful He did! Amen.

THE HONOR THAT BELONGS TO HIM

Give to the Lord the honor that belongs to Him.
Worship the Lord in the beauty of holy living.
PSALM 29:2 NLV

Maybe you have family members in the military. People treat them with great respect and offer thanks for their service. They are honored for what they do.

Some people work hard to earn the respect of others. They work as nurses, doctors, teachers, police officers, and so forth. But there is One who doesn't have to work to earn your respect. He's already got it, because it belonged to Him in the first place!

All of the honor belongs to God! And He wants you to worship Him, simply because He's worthy.

Now, think about all of those occupations once more: military, nurse, doctor, teacher, police officer. . .notice anything they have in common? They're all service workers, people who live to serve others. That is the key, girl! They deserve honor because, like your Creator, they live to serve. And you can live to serve too. No matter what you do for a living, you can become more like Jesus, the ultimate servant!

I give You honor, just for being who You are, Lord! Amen.

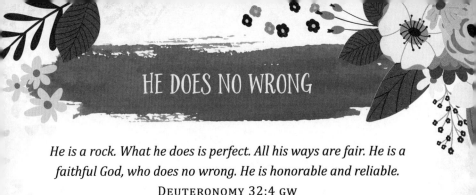

HE DOES NO WRONG

He is a rock. What he does is perfect. All his ways are fair. He is a
faithful God, who does no wrong. He is honorable and reliable.
DEUTERONOMY 32:4 GW

Today's verse is so powerful, and it can only be used to describe one person, your heavenly Father. Who else could be called a rock? Who else is perfect? Who else is always fair? Who else is always faithful? Who else does no wrong? Who else displays honor and reliability at all times? Only God. He's in a class of His own! No one even comes close.

When you need a rock (a defender), call on Him.

When others let you down, He never will.

When others treat you unfairly, He's 100 percent fair.

When others are unfaithful, He's sticking with you till the end.

This is your trustworthy, holy Father. And best of all, He created you, His worthy daughter, to be like Him. So do your best to live up to these high standards. Be fair. Be faithful. Be honorable. Be reliable. In other words, be just like Him.

I want to be more like You, Jesus! Help me, I pray. Amen.

BECAUSE HE'S WORTHY

The high and honored One Who lives forever, Whose name is Holy, says, "I live in the high and holy place. And I also live with those who are sorry for their sins and have turned from them and are not proud. I give new strength to the spirit of those without pride, and also to those whose hearts are sorry for their sins."
ISAIAH 57:15 NLV

Maybe you've heard the expression, "She's too big for her britches!" It's a southern saying that means you're too high and mighty for your own good. You think too much of yourself.

Now think of that expression in light of today's Bible verse. God is the high and honored One, far exalted above any of us here on earth. And yet He didn't think it was beneath Him to come to earth, live as a man, and die a sinner's death on a cross.

Why would someone so high, so holy, stoop so low? Why would Jesus live among sinners and even die for them?

Love propelled Him here! Love brought Him to earth. Love placed Him squarely in the middle of messed-up humanity. And love has placed you here too! So never be too proud, too puffed up, to associate with those who make mistakes. Be like Jesus. Love the broken.

I'll be like You, Jesus! Amen.

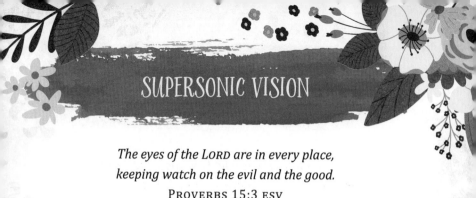

SUPERSONIC VISION

The eyes of the LORD are in every place,
keeping watch on the evil and the good.
PROVERBS 15:3 ESV

God has supersonic X-ray vision. He sees what's going on across the globe and can keep track of it all at the same time! He can see inside of a prison cell in America while viewing a child's broken heart in India. He sees the senior citizen struggling to live alone in South America and the hungry, homeless woman who lives in Africa.

He sees it all, and He cares about it all. (How could He not care? It must break His heart to witness the brokenness of humanity.)

Who else do you know with supersonic vision like this? Who else sees across the globe and inside of the human heart? No one. Only God! And He's watching over you, girl. He loves you so much, cares about you so deeply, that His eyes are on you, making sure you're well provided for and safe. What a tender, loving, worthy Father!

I want eyes to see like You do, Lord! Make me more like You, I pray. I don't want to overlook anyone. Amen.

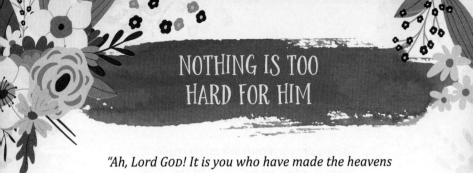

NOTHING IS TOO HARD FOR HIM

"Ah, Lord GOD! It is you who have made the heavens and the earth by your great power and by your outstretched arm! Nothing is too hard for you."
JEREMIAH 32:17 ESV

Think of the hardest math problem you've ever tried to solve. Did it drive you crazy until you figured it out? Now think of the biggest family problem you've ever faced. Did you finally get past it?

Life is filled with problems and complications, and many of them will seem impossible to you. When you reach the point where things are beyond your capabilities, never forget that God is capable. What you cannot do, He can. Nothing is too hard for Him. There's no problem too big for Him. He can solve every one.

He created the heavens and the earth. That should convince you that He knows how things work. And because He knows how they work, He knows how to fix them when they're broken. You can trust Him when you're going through stuff, girl. He won't let you down. That's a promise.

You're the great Fixer, Lord! I'm glad You're able, even when I am not. Amen.

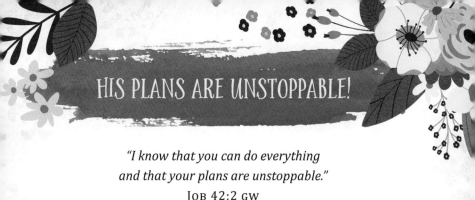

HIS PLANS ARE UNSTOPPABLE!

"I know that you can do everything
and that your plans are unstoppable."
JOB 42:2 GW

Your heavenly Father is unstoppable! He's like that Energizer Bunny. . .He keeps going and going. You? Not so much! You don't always have a lot of perseverance, but He does.

He never stops caring, never stops working, never stops loving, no matter what. Your heavenly Father is on the job twenty-four seven, 365 days a year. Best of all, He never gives up on you, even when you give up on yourself. When you don't see yourself as worthy, He does. When you don't see yourself as lovable, He does! He's a persistent, never-say-never Father, and He's ready to pour out that same persistence on you, His daughter.

If you want to live an unstoppable life, then becoming more like Him is important. When you feel like giving up—on life, on relationships, on your crazy schoolwork—remember, He's unstoppable. And because you're created in His image, you can be unstoppable too! Never forget, He is worthy of your praise. And girl, He calls you worthy too!

Lord, You're simply amazing. I don't have words to describe You, but I choose to praise You today because You alone are worthy! Thanks for all You do. Amen.

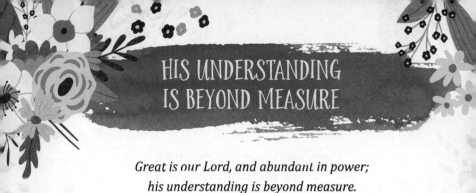

HIS UNDERSTANDING IS BEYOND MEASURE

Great is our Lord, and abundant in power;
his understanding is beyond measure.
PSALM 147:5 ESV

He gets it. That thing you're worrying about? God gets it. He understands. He sees all and knows all.

Now ponder this for a moment. On the other side of the planet there's a woman who's struggling to feed her family. She doesn't speak your language. You have nothing in common. But God gets her too. He understands her situation, and He cares.

He gets that man who is agonizing over losing his job. He understands that elderly woman in the hospital bed who wonders if she'll die alone. He gets the yard worker, slaving away in the heat to care for someone else's lawn. He understands all of them. He knows where they're coming from, what they're going through, even what they're thinking. (Wow!)

Your heavenly Father is all-knowing, all-powerful, and filled with love and compassion for all of creation. His love knows no limits. His knowledge knows no bounds. Now that's a God who's worthy to be praised!

I can't even fathom how You know all of that, Lord! But I'm in awe of You, for sure. Amen.

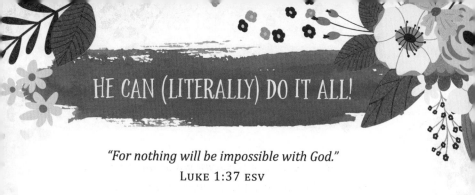

HE CAN (LITERALLY) DO IT ALL!

"For nothing will be impossible with God."
LUKE 1:37 ESV

If someone asked you to make a list of all the things that would be impossible for you to do, what would you write down first? Maybe you'd add things like: *Fly to the moon. Disappear. Time travel.* The list would go on and on! The truth is, there are *w-a-y* too many things we humans simply can't do.

Now think about God's amazing abilities. All of those things we can't do, He can. Every single one. In fact, you can't think of a thing that He's unable to do. (He's pretty amazing, isn't He?)

Now do you see why He's worthy to be praised? If you're sick, He can heal you. If you're hungry, He can feed you. If you need clothing, He can clothe you. If you're lonely, He will sweep in and be a friend to you. If you're in need of anything at all, He will meet your need if you ask.

Now that you know God is capable of all of these things, what's keeping you from asking for what you need? Get to it, girl!

Lord, You're worthy! Only You are capable of, well, everything! I'm amazed by You. Amen.

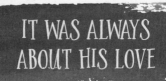

IT WAS ALWAYS ABOUT HIS LOVE

He is the radiance of the glory of God and the exact imprint of his nature, and he upholds the universe by the word of his power. After making purification for sins, he sat down at the right hand of the Majesty on high.
HEBREWS 1:3 ESV

Jesus is worthy, sweet girl. And because He's worthy, His gift of salvation has made you worthy. What a gift!

You'll make mistakes, sure. You'll mess up every day. You're still human. But because of His worthiness and His compassionate nature, you'll get a second chance. And a third. And a fourth. Tomorrow will be better. And you'll keep growing and getting closer to Him in the years ahead.

But here's the truth: your worthiness was never based on your actions. You're His kid, and He made you worthy the day He adopted you into the family. So enjoy your relationship with the One who thinks you hung the moon! (You are pretty special, you know!)

Jesus, thank You! I love being Your daughter. I feel like such a mess-up sometimes, but You're so forgiving and gracious to me. Even on days when I don't feel worthy at all, You remind me that all You ever wanted from me was my heart. It's Yours, totally and completely. Amen.

SCRIPTURE INDEX

OLD TESTAMENT

MORE INSPIRATION FOR YOUR HEART!

YOU MATTER

This delightful devotional, created just for teen girls like you, is a beautiful reminder of your purpose. . .your worth. . .your place in the world. 180 encouraging readings and inspiring prayers, rooted in biblical truth, will reassure your doubting heart. In each devotional reading, you will encounter the bountiful love and grace of your Creator, while coming to understand His plan—for you and you alone.

Flexible Casebound / 978-1-64352-520-4 / $12.99